LIFE LESSONS

Reaching Teenagers through Literature

LIFE LESSONS

Reaching Teenagers through Literature

by

DAVID SLOAN

Printed with support from the Waldorf Curriculum Fund

Published by:
Waldorf Publications at the
Research Institute for Waldorf Education
38 Main Street
Chatham, NY 12037

Title: *Life Lessons: Reaching Teenagers through Literature*
Author: David Sloan
Editor: David Mitchell
Proofreader: Ann Erwin
Cover: Hallie Wootan
© 2007 by AWSNA
ISBN # 978-1-888365-90-0

Contents

Introduction: Twice-warming Words 7

An Antidote to Technology 13
    The Technology Highway
    The Waldorf Alternative
    The Power of Ideals
    A Developmental Curriculum

Ninth Grade: Posing the Polarities 23
    Riding the Roller Coaster
    Comedy and Tragedy
    Schooling the Imagination
    Building Confidence through Grammar
    Teaching the Novel
    Other Ninth Grade Readings

Tenth Grade: Logic and Lawfulness 57
    The Oddest Sea: Teaching *The Odyssey*
    The Art of Poetry: Developing Imagination, Inspiration,
        and Intuition
    Student Poetry: Windows into the Teenage Soul
    The Bible as Source of Literature: From Love of the
        Law to the Law of Love

Eleventh Grade: The Journey towards Selfhood 79
    The Dark Night of the Soul
    Gilgamesh: The Story of Becoming Human
    Dante's *Divine Comedy*: Sins of Fire, Sins of Ice
    Parzival: The Quest within the Question
    Hamlet: The First Modern Individual
    The Tempest: Virtue Rather than Vengeance
    The Romantic Poets: Seeing into the Life of Things

Twelfth Grade: Song of Myself, Song of the World 135
    Straddling a Great Threshold
    The Birth of American Literature
    Goethe's *Faust*: Encounter with Evil
    Russian Literature: Regaining the Spirit through Suffering
    A Final Lesson: The Power of Transformation

Bibliography 186

Dedication 190

Introduction

Twice-warming Words

Firewood, goes the adage, can warm us twice—once from the splitting and once from the fire. Over the years, I have found that literature provides a similar double blessing—first in the initial reading and again in the teaching. When I was around ten years old, the Greek myths, particularly the labors of Hercules, stirred my imagination deeply. The magical activity of reading turned the words on the page first into windows, then into doors; they invited me inside the story. I became the valiant figure cleaning the Augean stables, the hero grappling with the Nemean lion. About that same time, I began to devour the Clair Bee's Chip Hilton sports series. No one would classify these books as great literature, and yet they had a profound effect on me during my formative years. Through most of my adolescence, I wanted to be like Chip Hilton—not only the exceptional three-sport athlete, but also the upright individual who stood up to bullies, stood behind his friends, and delivered in the clutch.

After I became an educator, teaching literature had the same kindling effect, both for me and for my students. This was never more apparent than during my early teaching days at the Green Meadow Waldorf School. Just before arriving at Green Meadow in my late twenties, I had been working in a residential school in the mountains of southern California for troubled teenagers, kids with a history of drug and alcohol abuse, self-esteem problems, family abuse/neglect problems. After four years of intense work, and after my wife got pregnant, we decided we wanted to raise our family in the sheltering embrace of a Waldorf school environment. So we visited a number of schools on the West and East Coasts, with Green Meadow Waldorf School in Spring Valley, New York, as one of our stops.

On the day that I visited, I sat in on a sixth grade Geology main lesson. There was no formal announcement that I was a candidate to be next year's class teacher, but this was a very savvy class, and they knew why I was there. Despite my presence, or maybe because of it, the class was like every teacher's worse nightmare. The teacher was a kindly older fellow, who was trying his best to interest his charges in the world of crystals. Discipline was not his forte. He was drawing geometrical shapes on the board with his back to the class, while the students were running amok—chipping off pieces of crystal that were being passed around the room and throwing them at each other or carving with them into the desk tops, reading comic books, wrestling in the back of the room trying to push one another out the open window, chatting idly with each other, absolutely oblivious to what the teacher was doing at the front of the room. At the end of the class, one of the boys who had been most obnoxious sidled up to me and asked, "What did you think of our class? We were on our best behavior." And the only answer I could think of at the time was, "So was I."

From that moment the gauntlet was thrown down, and for some perverse, unexplainable reason, I was drawn to teaching this particular group of hooligans. I believed in some arrogant way that I was more than a match for these twenty-seven brash and swaggering thirteen-year-olds. After all, hadn't I just spent four years working with far more difficult kids—drug addled, sexually abused, criminally inclined delinquents? How wrong I was. After two weeks trying to teach them English grammar—actually, to be honest, after two weeks of just trying to get their attention—I remember pedaling furiously home after school one day, welling up with tears of fury. Individually these seventh graders were exceedingly bright and responsive, but as a class they were a mob—relentlessly rude, lacking any sense of discipline or respect. That night I called a few parents, who were also desperate for me to avoid becoming another in a long line of teachers who had been driven out of teaching by this class. I warned these parents that I was going to send several of their sons and daughters home the next day at the slightest provocation and asked for their support.

The next morning the showdown didn't take long to materialize. As soon as the customary din started and the gabbing and ignoring the teacher occurred, I shocked three of the worst offenders by sending them out after telling them that I was calling their parents to pick them up and that they were to stay home until they were ready to be respectful and attentive in class. At this, the predictable uproar from the other students in the class began to crescendo, with outcries such as, "You can't do that! That's not fair! If you send them home, we're going too!"

Now I must admit that I was somewhat fearful of this last possibility. If all of the students in the class had walked out in solidarity and support for their three scapegoated classmates, that probably would have ended a promising teaching career. Instead of writing this, I might be hauling concrete blocks or chickens across Kansas. Thankfully, only five of them actually walked out—I told them to stay home as well under the same conditions—and, after the smoke cleared, I actually had a main lesson where the students acknowledged my right to stand before them and teach them.

I wish I could say that from that day on, I turned into Moses and the seventh graders the Israelites about to enter the Promised Land. We did reach an uneasy truce, with occasional flare-ups along the way. We didn't really turn a definitive corner until the spring, when it came time to do a play. The year before, not surprisingly, they had taken great delight in performing *Julius Caesar*, who, as you may remember, was an archetypal authority figure assassinated by supposedly loyal underlings. My choice was *The Miracle Worker*, the story about blind, deaf and spoiled wild child Helen Keller and her tenacious teacher Annie Sullivan.

At the risk of sounding self-congratulatory, I want to emphasize how the choice of this particular story changed the nature of the class and their relationship to their teachers. Of course, enacting *The Miracle Worker* onstage provided these young teenagers with an almost visceral experience of Helen's challenges. One should never underestimate the power of the theater to work its magic on both audience and actors. However, in this case I would credit the story itself for helping to transform a class of undisciplined, willful teenagers into a still spirited, but ever more purposeful and compliant class.

Helen Keller's struggle and ultimate breakthrough was a journey out of nearly absolute darkness and into a new world of meaning. Even self-involved seventh graders, whose deepest questions on occasion seem to be "How do I look?" and "When's supper?" found themselves deeply touched by Helen's groping to find meaning in her life. Sometimes there is no greater awakener for these young people flailing about, without much sense of direction or purpose, than the realization that there are people worse off than they are, people in dire need. All it takes to ignite that smoldering idealism of youth is to make them aware of the injustice such people suffer or the tribulations they must overcome.

For Annie Sullivan, words were the keys to bringing light into Helen Keller's life. Towards the end of *The Miracle Worker*, before the final breakthrough at the water pump, Annie expresses perfectly what has become my inspiration for becoming, and remaining, an educator.

> I wanted to teach you—oh, everything the earth is full of, Helen, everything on it that's ours for a wink and it's gone, and what we are on it, the—light we bring to it and leave behind in—words, why, you can see five thousand years back in a light of words, everything we feel, think, know—and share in words, so not a soul is in darkness, or

done with, even in the grave. And I know, I know, one word and I can—put the world in your hands—and whatever it is to me, I won't take less.[1]

Over the years I have witnessed the power of literature to quicken the minds and fortify the hearts of young people hungry for soul nourishment. Whether the story possesses the epic scale of Herman Melville's *Moby Dick*, the dramatic intensity of Lorraine Hansberry's *A Raisin in the Sun*, or the lyrical expressiveness of Samuel Taylor Coleridge's "Kubla Khan," literature can offer teenagers more than material for the standard academic exercises of character analysis and thematic discussion. Literature can speak to adolescents' innermost needs to learn about themselves, about their relationships, about the human condition. These time-transcending stories provide young people with "life lessons," if they can only learn to recognize the wisdom imbedded in the words.

An Antidote to Technology

The Technology Highway

Education in America today stands at a crossroads. Down one road, technological marvels offer the promise of a future largely defined by machines, with all their clever, labor-saving advances, conveniences and amusements. However, as gleaming as that highway appears, I wonder if it will be a real or a "virtual" road. Will direct, first-hand experiences—a trip to a local soup kitchen to lend a hand, a hike during an optics class to a pond to observe the effects of light in water, a theater outing to see the play the students have just read—be considered quaint but outmoded activities? Will they all too soon be supplanted by sophisticated computer models and flashy video simulations?

The other road has actual people traveling along its lanes. Instead of sleek machines whizzing along at blinding speeds, these people may be biking or walking, taking the time to notice the terrain, reading the signs placed every so often to commemorate some significant events, stopping at picnic tables and at turnouts to appreciate spectacular vistas. On this road the journey is as important as the destination. Here progress makes room for process, quantity defers to quality, and values attract more attention than video games.

Outwardly, it appears that the technology highway is the preferred route these days. The educational landscape has changed greatly in recent years. The proliferation of electronic media has undeniably altered many of today's classrooms. Instead of using pen and paper, many students in public and private schools take notes by tapping away on laptop computers. They pass notes by surreptitiously sending text messages on cleverly pocketed cell phones. To do research they forego time-consuming library trips by clicking on any of countless internet sites.

Champions of the new technology point triumphantly to the advantages today's students enjoy over their counterparts of a generation ago. These technologically adept young people have unparalleled, almost instantaneous access to more information than anyone could have imagined even ten years ago. They can communicate at nearly the speed of light, through printed or spoken word, with anyone around the globe as long as that person is similarly equipped. They can amuse themselves endlessly through the wonders of electronic wizardry, with an array of iPods, wide screen televisions, x-box video games, cell phones, and computers that can download favorite movies, television programs and songs.

This last development should give us pause. In 1985, Neil Postman began his groundbreaking book *Amusing Ourselves to Death* with a Foreword that contrasts the nightmarish visions of Orwell's *1984* and Huxley's *Brave New World,* both written in the middle of the last century. While much of the world worried about Orwell's depiction of an external, totalitarian regime that could crush individual freedoms, Postman pointed more urgently and emphatically at Huxley's dystopia, especially at people's mindless pursuit of pleasure. "Orwell feared we would become a captive culture. Huxley feared we would become a trivial culture. ...In *1984* people are controlled by inflicting pain. In *Brave New World*, they are controlled by inflicting pleasure."[2]

Twenty years later, Postman is looking increasingly like a prophet. The diversions offered by the allure of electronic media have captivated today's youth. Indeed, one of the biggest changes in the past decade has been the number of hours young people devote to "screen time." One recent study conducted by the National Institute on Media and the Family estimated that children spend approximately 44.5 hours per week in front of one screen or another, an average of over six hours per day.

Yet the virtual realities with which these young people have become so enamored do not appear to be preparing them for the actual challenges of real life. Although not conclusive, many ongoing studies link the increase in screen time to the alarming rise in obesity, sleeplessness, violence and attention-deficit disorders among our youth. For all their access to a cyber-universe of information, for all the instant modes of communication available, for all their expertise about information technology, young people today still have to face the same outer uncertainties and inner tempests that teenagers always have.

I would contend that these children of the computer age are *less* well-equipped than past generations to successfully deal with life's trials. The ease and speed with which a savvy computer user can zip through cyberspace is rarely duplicated in real life. How do individuals used to instant access deal with the growing impatience of waiting in snarled traffic? Are hours of mindless diversions the best training for thoughtful discourse in a classroom or creative thinking in the workplace? Can the faceless contacts of chat rooms and text messaging possibly prepare young people to navigate the intimacies and complexities of real-life relationships? As David Elkind puts it, "While many teenagers are sophisticated users of technology, they remain as naïve as preceding generations about the human condition."[3]

Where can young people turn to learn about the "human condition"? The traditional sources of what we might call moral education have lost some of their cache. With the fragmentation of family life and the decline of formal religious training, people are looking more urgently than ever to schools to fill the "values gap." Yet public schools have gone another direction. Driven by the "No Child Left Behind" policies of the current administration, public educators increasingly use scripted curricula to instruct students in test-taking techniques, virtually ignoring the teaching of values. On the other end of the spectrum, the upsurge of interest in values-laden religious schools has ignited a public furor. Many critics question whether a curriculum based primarily on ancient, sacred texts, such as the Bible or the Talmud or the Koran—a curriculum that also sidesteps much of contemporary scientific theory—can adequately prepare young people for the modern world.

The Waldorf Alternative

Between these divergent models—between exclusively secular and exclusively religious approaches to education—Waldorf education offers another alternative. Rudolf Steiner, founder of the first Waldorf school in Stuttgart, Germany, in 1919, spoke compellingly about creating an educational model that both inculcated morality *and* prepared young people for life. However, he also understood that one should never mistake sermonizing for moral education, especially when teaching teenagers.

> If I give a child moral precepts, I make morality distasteful, disgusting, to him, and this fact plays an important part in modern social life. You have no idea how much disgust human beings have felt for some of the most beautiful, the noblest, the most majestic of man's moral impulses because they have been presented to them in the form of precepts, in the form of intellectual ideas.[4]

How, then, can Waldorf teachers teach morality without resorting to deadly preaching? In every section of the school the Waldorf "secret" is the same, even if the secret is "revealed" differently at each age level. In the nursery/kindergarten, moral education issues from the bearing of the teachers, from the songs they sing, from the mood of reverence they create and, most especially, from the stories they tell. In the elementary school, from the fairy tales of first grade to the in-depth biographies of great men and women in eighth grade, once again stories convey the moral forces that imprint their lessons deeply into the children. At the high school level, the classics of literature, poetry, and drama provide the stories that can speak to teenagers' deepest longings. What is great literature if not an expression of great authors' strivings to convey what it means to be human?

Of course, Waldorf teachers do not have a monopoly on the classics, or the transcendentalists, or Shakespeare. So what distinguishes a Waldorf high school curriculum from other educational models? One difference can be traced to the vision a Waldorf faculty carries of the young people they teach. How teachers educate teenagers depends largely on how the former view this tumultuous phase of life. Some mainstream educators see adolescence as less than it really is, as some simmering rebellion which needs to be quelled before it runs amok, or as an "illness" that only time can cure. Still others consider the high school years simply as a time of "training," the test-taking model employed exclusively as a preparation for college or the workplace. It is not surprising, then, that our high schools begin to resemble either armed camps—complete with guards, windowless classrooms, and security devices at every entrance—or treatment centers or obedience schools.

Waldorf high school teachers, however, view adolescence as something more than it appears. We recognize that young people are spiritual beings, with ripening capacities to think more penetratingly, to feel more deeply, and to act more decisively than ever before. In the teenage years a profound transformation takes place and powerful inner forces for the future are unleashed. Only in the first years of life do children change more dramatically than in their teenage years. In adolescence, for the first time, young people consciously begin to forge their own identities and to fashion their own values. They have inklings of what may become lifelong aspirations. Perhaps at no other time do teenagers awaken so intensely to feelings simultaneously painful and exhilarating, feelings about something familiar dying within and of a whole new interior world being born.

What is dying? The innocence of childhood is fading away. Adolescence is often represented in some circles by the biblical image of the expulsion from the Garden of Eden. This is indeed a true picture of the dying away of the "paradise consciousness" of childhood. It doesn't happen all at once. In "Ode: Intimations of Immortality," William Wordsworth describes the "prison bars" that begin to close around us already from the moment of birth. By puberty this paradise that was childhood, with the endless days of play, the fertile fantasy life, the lack of self-consciousness, seems but a faraway dream. The loss of the buoyancy and brightness of childhood can turn the teenage years into a period of mourning.

What is being born? On the more obvious, biological level, they rather suddenly transform from being children to being capable of conceiving children themselves. Just as mysteriously, they also experience another birth: in their thinking, a new capacity to conceive abstract ideas. Any of us who have survived raising teenage sons/daughters know that these new cognitive faculties are very much like a two-edged sword. A sword severs. Our thinking separates us from the world so we can see it ever more clearly. Rightly developed, it becomes the vehicle for apprehending the loftiest of ideals. It can also become a stinging, critical weapon. Teenagers want to change the world, and they want to begin with you and me. This is why we teachers and parents feel as if we are being dissected under a microscope when we find ourselves in the presence of a withering, newly critical teenage gaze. I have learned to not take it too personally when one of my students says to me, as happened last year, "Mr. Sloan, did you know that your teeth are too small for your face?"

Several years ago, my then fourteen-year-old daughter begged her mother not to speak to her friends. "Why, did I say something wrong?" my wife asked, to which my daughter replied, "One of them noticed that your nose moves when you talk. That is SO humiliating!" We need to understand that their constant critiques are born of the highest ideals. When they see these woefully flawed grownups around them, they can't help themselves; they are simply trying to improve us.

Thankfully, young people experience a third birth in adolescence, one that arises out of teenagers' feeling life. They begin to develop the capacity for real love. That's not to say that younger children don't love their parents or their pet turtles. But instead of a largely unconscious sympathy for the things in their world, teenagers become acutely aware of their own incompleteness and feel the first stirrings of love as a way of entering consciously into a communion with another human being. Waldorf educators see in adolescence a convergence of two archetypal human experiences: the loss of childhood with its charmed innocence, and the birth of adulthood with its potential for critical thinking, mature judgment and responsible action. The high school teacher, then, must be both a midwife and a grief counselor, attending to the births and to the dyings away that are occurring in the students.

The Power of Ideals

In the midst of these traumatic changes, teenagers are also beginning to inwardly experience the galvanizing power of ideals. Rudolf Steiner wrote that ideals are to a child's soul at this time of life what the skeleton is to the body—nothing less than the scaffolding that the young person needs for stability and strength and direction. It is so interesting that Steiner draws this parallel between ideals and the skeleton—for it is only at puberty that children begin to actually experience their own skeletal systems, as the bones in their limbs lengthen and thicken during the dramatic growth spurts so characteristic of this age. Just as the loss of the milk teeth around age six or seven signals the readiness of children to start formal schooling, so this descent into the skeleton signals a new readiness to embrace ideals, to explore their own inner latitudes, to think more penetratingly than ever before.

Adolescents often express these ideals as longings, sometimes voiced, but more often unexpressed. More than thirty years of teaching have led me to a somewhat surprising conclusion: Despite the outer transformations wrought by technology, teenagers have not changed inwardly so much. Clearly they have shorter attention spans, and sometimes it seems harder to engage their wills, but at their core, today's adolescents have the same longings that high school students did a generation ago.

- They crave meaning in their lives and in the larger world.
- They long for human relationships and a sense of relatedness to the wider world.
- They desire empowerment, a sense that they can make a difference in the world.

Finding meaning while growing up in our media-sodden culture is no easy task. I recently completed teaching a course to Green Meadow seniors on the Birth of American Literature. One of the first assignments was to fill a time capsule with several objects that represented core values of contemporary American culture. What did they come up with? A McDonald's happy meal, a credit card, a bottle of pills, the Constitution, a DVD/video and, for the first time, some kind of security system. Their choices were thoughtful but very distressing. Many of these young people see the world they are about to enter as a place where instant gratification is valued over measured, deliberate progress towards long-term goals, where consumerism is king, where mindless entertainment feeds us on superficialities, and where fear casts a pall over what would normally be considered opportunities. In such a landscape, where, indeed, can young people find meaning?

Their second hunger—for relationship—arises out of a double detachment. On the cultural level, it is obvious that we live in an age when people interact more and more with technological gadgets and less and less with people. Just try talking to a real human being when you want an explanation of your wireless phone bill. As already stated, all the cell phones, internet connections and satellite television stations offer expanded information-sharing and entertainment possibilities, but is the net effect of all this technology going to enhance or degrade our human experience?

On a more personal level, the heretofore-mentioned pain of adolescent angst and alienation is compounded by this technological assault. Childhood might be thought of as a time of natural sympathy, a feeling of warmth for the things of this world;

the gesture that comes to mind is that of an embrace. However, these new feelings of antipathy, represented by a hard, hands-off gesture that pushes the world away, begin to awaken teenagers to the growing separation between their precious inner life and the reality of what's "out there." In their growing isolation, adolescents crave the warmth and affirmation that relationships can bring.

The third hunger—for empowerment—is most under attack. At its worst, our sedentary culture promotes a kind of paralysis of the will. One of the most disheartening utterances to come out the mouths of teenagers is to hear them say, "Why vote? What difference does it make? Nothing ever changes anyway." Adolescence should be the phase of life when flaming ideals light up most incandescently, when young people can't wait to change the world. So why is it that teenagers today seem more susceptible than ever to a kind of ennui or hopelessness? It is distressing that one of the favorite catch phrases of young people frustrated in their quest for empowerment today is ... "Whatever."

What can be particularly frustrating for young people in conventional school settings is that these longings can seem mutually exclusive during their adolescence. Pursuit of superficial experiences can lead to relationships that lack real substance or meaning, while the so-called "meanings" they are taught in school can lack coherence or relatedness. As a result, they can feel adrift, alienated, and vaguely thwarted in their pursuit of selfhood.

A Developmental Curriculum

Addressing those three ideals lies at the very heart of the Waldorf high school literature curriculum. Teachers consider every text, every poem that they select in the light of the soul nourishment it might provide the students. Here we arrive at a second distinguishing characteristic of Waldorf education: its developmental character. Most educational systems pay little heed to what we might call the lawful unfolding of human life. They view adolescence as a single stage of life, or they lump teenagers into broad categories—13 to 18, 15 to 19. However, anyone who has interacted with teenagers knows that most fourteen-year-old high school freshmen are virtually a different species when compared to, say, eighteen-year-old seniors. Ninth graders lack the cognitive facility, the emotional depth, and the self-possession of their older classmates. Conducting English classes with freshmen and seniors sitting side-by-side would be doing a disservice to both. Of course, not all young people go through their stages of growth at precisely the same time; one can find exceptionally mature ninth graders, as well as atypically childish twelfth graders. Yet in general, most adolescents undergo inner psychological changes—one might even call them soul transformations—at roughly the same stages. Waldorf teachers experience these sometimes subtle, sometimes dramatic changes from year to year and strive to create a curriculum that meets students' needs.

This developmental approach is, along with the higher vision teachers carry of their students, perhaps the most defining feature of the Waldorf model. Hermann Baravalle, one of the pioneers of Waldorf education in America, summarized this idea: "Describe objectively the processes of growth in the consciousness of the child and you describe the plan of the school."[5] The aim of this book is to characterize both the general stages of consciousness that young people experience during their high school years and some of the literature that we have found that fortifies and enlarges our students in their journey towards selfhood.

Ninth Grade:
Posing the Polarities

Riding the Roller Coaster

If the Waldorf curriculum is to reflect the needs of the students in their gradual unfolding, then we must examine closely each particular stage of a young person's growth. Instead of arbitrarily deciding to teach this science course or that piece of literature, we take our cues from the inner requirements of the students themselves, and then shape the program accordingly. What, then, is the experience of many ninth graders? Most have already reached puberty and are in the throes of their newfound powers. They find themselves in possession of a teeming inner realm that seems to control them more often than they control it. Parents who have raised a fourteen- or fifteen-year-old know that it is akin to living in an amusement park, with the roller coaster constantly whirling around the house. Teenagers at this age are by their very nature extremists, swinging from giddiness to depression, from dreamy unawareness to acute attention within the space of seconds. However, it is probably important here to differentiate between male and female students, since the gap is often so great between them that they appear to belong to different species.

For a couple of years at least, it seems as if the gods stack the odds in favor of the girls. As the girls themselves will so readily explain, they are simply more mature than the boys when they enter the high school, and of course they are right. The girls come into ninth grade so ready to dive into and share their burgeoning inner world, while the boys seem somewhat bewildered by all the changes they are undergoing. Steiner explains the huge gender gap at this age in spiritual terms. He points to the incipient ego forces in females that permeate the feeling life of girls—also referred to as the astral body—at this age. This absorption of ego forces into the feeling realm intensifies girls' awareness of the depth and potency of their emotions. So strongly can girls feel their newfound blend of passion, power and discernment that they can become emboldened to the point of sassiness. By contrast, Steiner suggests that the ego forces of the boys penetrate less into their feelings than into their physical natures. That may help explain that while the girls become so enamored of and so interested in talking about relationships, in writing feverishly in their secret diaries and fantasizing about saving all the homeless children in Calcutta, or at least about marrying Johnny Depp (a fantasy they share with my wife), the boys are still out on the playing field punching each other and giving one other wedgies.

Ninth grade boys can appear to be crude dullards when compared to their female counterparts, by whom they are often dwarfed, sometimes even in stature as well as in sheer overpowering emotional intensity. The girls seem so intent upon confronting life, while the boys would just as soon hide themselves away until they are better armed. Jaimen McMillan, founder of the Spatial Dynamics program in this country, once described this stage of male adolescence by saying that they might as well wear a sign during this time that says simply, "Under Construction," like those building sites that are all boarded up with barbed wire strung around the top. Thankfully, this gap usually closes by eleventh grade. As one of the feistier boys once remarked to a girl who, for the umpteenth time, had just pointed out the how much more mature girls were than boys, "Sure, you girls are more mature for a little while, until the boys pass you by as juniors while you stagnate where you are for the rest of your lives!" Despite their differences, both boys and girls at this age live in the polarities of their mood swings, and that is what they meet in the ninth grade curriculum.

Comedy and Tragedy

One of the central courses freshmen experience is called Comedy and Tragedy. We begin the block with the very origins of drama. We have them read a Greek tragedy, a Shakespearean comedy, and a modern play. Our aims are threefold: (1) to guide ninth graders through the physical development of the theater, from its earliest incarnations as crude amphitheaters in ancient Greece to the experimental "black boxes" in today's high-tech theater complexes; (2) to gently introduce students in a simplified form, to the evolution of human consciousness; and (3) to present, through the polarity of tragedy and comedy, a reflection of ninth graders' own inner polarities.

Why emphasize the development of the actual, theatrical stages, as opposed to, say, psychological or literary innovations? Ninth graders seem to need physical "grounding," and any references to the material world have an anchoring, reassuring quality that the students appreciate. So they learn about the original *orchestra*, which was Greek for *dancing place*—that open, circular area at the bottom of a hill where, at seasonal festivals, followers of Dionysus would act out scenes from his life and death. Behind the orchestra stood a makeshift tent—*skene* in Greek, which spawned the English word *scene*. As the skene evolved into first a wooden, then a stone structure that served as a backstage area, actors would exit and enter wearing different *personae*, or *masks,* to portray different characters.

The introduction of the original Greek terms can often stimulate thought-provoking discussions. The students see immediately that *persona* is obviously related to our word *personality*. Then they dig into the etymology of the word *character* and discover that it originally meant *to carve* or *to engrave*. When I ask the students what the difference is between one's personality and one's character, some can distinguish between the more superficial "mask-like" qualities that one's personality can present to the world and the more deeply "engraved," permanent qualities denoted by one's character.

They also learn about Shakespeare's Globe Theater, with its balcony, twin pillars holding up the roof over the stage, the trap door, and the thrust stage itself. Actually, for over twenty years whenever students would discuss the unique features of the Globe, I would ask them what advantage that jutting stage might provide actors. I always imagined that such close proximity to the groundlings—those spectators who paid a penny to stand under the open sky around the stage—would afford actors much greater range in the delivery of their lines, even allowing them to whisper intimate words or love or conspirators' secret plans. That was before I traveled to England a few years ago with my son to attend a play at the newly constructed replica of the original Globe. During the performance of *A Winter's Tale,* it began to pour, as it commonly does in London. Fortunately we were sitting on the second level of the three-tiered, roofed galleries, no more than forty feet from the stage. However, the roaring, dripping rain was so loud that the actors had to scream all their lines to be heard, even Florizel's and Perdita's most private declarations of love. Since then, I have been able to more accurately share with students the Globe's relative merits and drawbacks.

The second goal of the course—touching upon the evolution of human consciousness—may sound initially a bit ambitious for ninth graders, especially if we are trying to ground them in the physical realities of drama. However, without becoming too philosophical or speculative here, we can point to a definite, even stark, transformation in consciousness when moving from a play such as Sophocles' *Oedipus Rex* to Shakespeare's *A Midsummer Night's Dream* and a contemporary piece such as the brilliant *A Raisin in the Sun.*

To avoid abstraction with younger high school students, I favor what I would call a "phenomenological approach to literature." For years my scientific colleagues have stressed the importance of beginning with concrete, observable experiments that allow the phenomena to speak, instead of starting with abstract theories and then bending the phenomena to support some hypothesis. The obvious advantage to this method is that it leaves students free to see the world as objectively as possible. With literature, our "phenomena" are the words on the page. Instead of jumping to some interpretive conclusions that the words may not support, it is far more pedagogical to stick to the text. From there, students can discover how the structure of a story or poem enhances the meaning, or they can chart what transformations take place in a character from the beginning of a play to the end.

Using this phenomenological approach, ninth graders can see that the relationship between the spiritual and human realms changes radically in the three plays mentioned above. In Sophocles' play, the gods are all-powerful, superseded only by the Fates. Through the oracle at Delphi, they have decreed that the curse on Oedipus' family line will lead inexorably to his murdering his father and marrying his mother. While no gods appear directly in the play, their majestic presence hovers over the entire action, and the characters almost seem to be their playthings. To compound their fateful coupling, in their ignorance Oedipus and his wife/mother Jocasta deride the words of the gods.

> *Jocasta:* Aha! Forecasts of the gods, where are you now?...
> *Oedipus:* So we are done
> With delving into Pythian oracles,
> This jangled mongering with birds on high.
> *Jocasta:* How can a man have scruples
> When it's only Chance that's king?
> There's nothing certain, nothing preordained...[6]

Yet ignorance is no excuse in a world where the sins of the ancestors are revisited upon the children. After the terrible truth surfaces, Jocasta hangs herself and Oedipus inflicts his own horrific punishment by gouging out his eyes. He pleads with the Thebans to cast him out of their city. As a final wish before self-imposed exile, he asks to see his children/sisters. The advice he gives them is a poignant plea for the moderation the father/brother could never find.

> My darling little ones, if you could only understand
> I'd tell you, oh, so many things!
> Let this suffice, a simple prayer:
> Abide in modesty so may you live
> The happy life your father did not have.[7]

Oedipus has acted rashly, arrogantly, impetuously; ninth graders cannot help but notice the nightmarish consequences for scoffing at the gods.

In *A Midsummer Night's Dream*, Shakespeare has turned the gods into very fallible fairies, who bicker over each other's indiscretions and fall in love with weavers-turned-jackasses and mistakenly apply love juice upon the wrong Athenian youth's eyes. They have descended from the lofty heights of Mount Olympus to frolic in the same woods peopled by lovers and tradesmen. Their meddling in human affairs leads to near-disastrous, delightfully laughable consequences. Except for their magical powers, there is little to distinguish these spirit sprites from their bumbling human counterparts.

By the twentieth century, objective reality of a divine realm has become an open question. In Lorraine Hansberry's *A Raisin in the Sun*, an African American family has aspirations of moving out of its inner city tenement. The problem is that each of the family members has a different idea of how to dispose of the $10,000 life insurance payment they receive after the death of Mama's husband. In a heated scene between Mama and her nearly grown-up daughter, Mama assures Beneatha:

> *Mama:* 'Course you going to be a doctor, honey, God willing
> *Beneatha*: God hasn't got a thing to do with it.
> *Mama:* Beneatha—that just wasn't necessary.
> *Beneatha:* Well—neither is God. I get sick of hearing about God.
> *Mama:* Beneatha!

> *Beneatha:* I mean it! I'm just tired of hearing about God all the time. What has He got to do with anything? Does He pay tuition?
> *Mama:* You 'bout to get your fresh little jaw slapped! ...
> *Beneatha:* Mama, you don't understand....I get tired of Him getting credit for all the tings [sic] the human race achieves through its own stubborn effort. There simply is no blasted God—there is only man and it is he who makes miracles.
>
> *(Mama absorbs this speech, studies her daughter and rises slowly and crosses to Beneatha and slaps her powerfully across the face. After there is only silence and the daughter drops her eyes from her mother's face.)*
>
> *Mama:* Now—you say after me, in my mother's house there is still God. In my mother's house there is still God.
> *Beneatha:* In my mother's house there is still God.[8]

Mama may have coerced Beneatha into speaking the words, but ninth graders wonder if Mama has compelled Beneatha's belief.

As the play progresses, near-tragedy strikes as Walter, Mama's son and Beneatha's older brother, squanders the money in an ill-advised scheme to buy a liquor store, imperiling Mama's dream of buying a house in an all-white suburb of Chicago. However, the source of this disaster is not the Fates' immutable curse or any intrusive fairies. It is the result of Walter's all-too-human, volatile combination of ambition and poor judgment. To make matters worse, Walter plans to accept an offer from their future all-white neighbors to buy back Mama's dream house and thus prevent a black family from moving into the area. Only Walter's eleventh hour discovery of pride—in himself, his family and his race—forestalls a complete catastrophe. Some in the audience might credit Mama's faith in a higher force for Walter's "conversion," but many others might share Beneatha's doubts about a God who, if such a Being exists at all, has made Him/Herself mighty scarce in the past few centuries. Although it is beyond the ken of most ninth graders, this modern theme of feeling "god-forsaken" can be taken up in the eleventh and twelfth grades in the studies of *Parzival* and *Hamlet* and *Faust*.

The third aim of this course is to have ninth graders experience a number of polarities. So we look at the physiological and psychological foundations of laughing and crying. We examine the classical characteristics that distinguish comedy from tragedy. We explore the archetypal contrasts of Dionysian and Apollonian elements in drama that trace their roots back to ancient Greek mystery centers. Students learn that drama emerges from the combination of the Apollonian value on reason, moderation, and form and the Dionysian preference for passion, excess, and inwardness. In the plays the freshmen recoil with horror at the tragedy of Oedipus and laugh with delight when, in *A Midsummer Night's Dream*, Bottom the Weaver is transformed into a jackass—an experience to which many of them can relate!

In this study of comedy and tragedy, the students can recognize, albeit subconsciously, the same polarity that they struggle with every day: this precarious balancing act between their fledgling subjective world within and their interest in the objective world without. One of the central tenets of Waldorf education is that the more these students experience polarities in their studies—in the plays they read, in the experiments they conduct, in the illustrations they draw—the less likely they will be to either collapse in upon themselves or lose themselves by being pulled prematurely out into the world. They may, in fact, come to a kind of equilibrium between the extremes as a result of meeting polarities in their studies. In a way, you could say that in this course, and virtually every other block these young people encounter, they experience a mini-initiation. At every stage of their growth, they cross a threshold and meet themselves as they meet the curriculum.

Of course we have to do what we can to help them really *meet* their subjects. Ninth graders have a tendency to look but not to see, to cock their heads but not to hear. Asking ninth graders to see something clearly is a little like asking them to wade into a pond with a container and the task of bringing back some clean drinking water. The problem is that their own movements stir up the bottom and muddy the very water they're trying to collect.

So throughout the year, we require that they observe the world around them in a most rigorous and precise manner. Observation requires an inner stillness, an alertness. In chemistry, they have to follow closely what happens when heat is place under a beaker of water. In art history they must draw reproductions of the great Greek sculptures or Renaissance masters, with their unparalleled blend of grace and beauty. Surely one of the antidotes to the debased and soulless media images of sexuality bombarding these young people is for them to study the beauty of the human form.

In English class they keep a daily journal. Each week we give them some theme, with the goal of having students describe, as lucidly and objectively as possible, cloud formations, views out windows, gadgets, acorns. We do not encourage what Waldorf students fresh out of the elementary school seem naturally drawn to—writing some whimsical story about elves and talking trees and moonlight woven out of silver. Rather, we expect only clear, dispassionate description. This is not some diabolical high school teacher plot to squeeze the imaginative juices out of our charges. On the contrary, we Waldorf teachers believe that cultivating these powers of observation settles the waters roiled by ninth graders and allows the possibility of clarity and creativity in their thinking. As Ralph Waldo Emerson wrote in his essay *Nature*, "Every object, rightly seen, unlocks a new faculty of soul."[9]

Schooling the Imagination

Exercising students' powers of observation is one of the most effective methods of helping to contain and refine the ninth graders' newly emerging feeling life. Another method has to with schooling the imagination. Some parents and educators, particularly in the

Waldorf world, might think that the cultivation of the imagination is the rightful domain of the elementary school. This stems from one of the great misunderstandings about high school education—the idea that once the faculties for abstract thinking emerge in adolescence, we now have to appeal solely to those capacities for abstraction. But just as Steiner asserted that you cannot teach morality to the younger child by preaching, he also declared, "We cannot deal with the intellect "intellectually. If a child is coming into the domain of logic at the age of puberty, we must develop imagery. If we can give them pictures so they receive images of the world and their meaning, then they will be held."[10]

The imaginative approach to education that we associate with the younger years cannot simply stop when our students become teenagers any more than we stop teaching art or handcrafts or music in the high school. In the literature we offer them, we can engage and cultivate their imaginations in compelling ways. Again, Sophocles' *Oedipus* provides a graphic example. The Greeks were all familiar with Oedipus' plight. They knew that despite his best efforts to avoid his fate, Oedipus would end up fulfilling the oracle. When the horrifying truth comes to light late in the play, a messenger comes running onstage to report the carnage.

> *Official:* Jocasta's gone, the Queen.
> *Chorus:* Unhappy lady! How?
> *Official:* Self-destroyed. The pain of it
> You shall be spared who were not there,
> and from my poor memory shall recount the struggles
> of that lost princess. The moment she had
> burst into the house—running through the doors
> demented—she made for the bridal bed,
> plunging her fingers through her hair;
> and slamming shut the doors behind her
> sobbed out Laius' name (so long dead),

recalling the night his love had bred his murderer
and left a mother making cursed children with her son.

"Unhappy bed!" she wailed, "twice wicked soil!
The father's seedbed nurtured for the mother's son!"
And then she killed herself. I don't know how.
The final act escaped our eyes—all fastened now
upon the raving Oedipus who broke upon us,
stamping up and down and shouting out: "A weapon, quick!
Where is the brideless bride? Find me that double breeding ground."

He smashes hollering through the double doors
breaking all its bolts and lunges in.
And there we saw her hanging, twisted, tangled,
from a halter-sight that wrings from him
a maddened cry. He frees the noose and lays the wretched
woman down, then—O hideous sequel—rips from off her
dress the golden brooches she was wearing, holds them up,
and rams them home right through his eyes.
"Wicked, wicked eyes!" he gasps, "You shall not see me nor
my shame—not see my present crime. Go dark,
for all time blind to what you never should have seen,
and—blind to those this heart has cried to see."

And as this dirge went up so did his hands to strike his
founts of sight, not once but many times. And all the while
his eyeballs gushed in bloody dew upon his beard... no, not
dew, no oozing drops—a spurt of black-ensanguined rain like
hail beat down. A coupled punishment upon a coupled sin:
husband and wife one flesh in their disaster; their happiness
of long ago—true happiness now turned to tears this day;
to ruin, death and shame; no evil absent by whatever cursed
name.

Chorus: Unhappy man! And is he still in pain?

Messenger: He shouts for the barriers to be unbarred
and he displayed to all of Thebes—his father's murderer, his
mother's—no, a word too foul to say
as if he means to cast himself adrift
not rot at home the curser and the cursed.
His strength is gone; he needs a helping hand;
his wound and weakness more than he can bear.
But you will see. The doors are opening, look:
such a sight that turns all loathing into tears.[11]

This description is among the most gruesome in dramatic literature, but that in and of itself is hardly reason for emphasizing it in our study of the play. Obviously, this scene evokes lots of grimacing and discomfort in the students. Yet beyond the visceral reaction students experience, usually one of them will ask the key question: Why is the entire scene reported, not enacted onstage? Ninth graders are quite amazed to discover that for all their preoccupation with all the various "cides"—patricide, infanticide, matricide—the Greeks made a point of not dramatizing violence onstage. And this usually leads to a lively discussion about the relative merits of the Greek approach, which allows the audience to imagine poor, deranged Jocasta hanging herself and Oedipus blinding himself, as opposed to some modern movie version that would bludgeon the audience with a graphic, slow-motion depiction of the blood spurting out of Oedipus' eyes like "black-ensanguined rain."

Even the most jaded, movie-saturated students can see that the issue here has to do with freedom—having the freedom to inwardly picture the scene according to our own sensibilities versus being a captive to someone else's imagination of the events that we are compelled to witness—and, by the way, then to carry around within us for the rest of our lives. I still have an image of those zombie-like aliens in *The Invasion of the Body Snatchers* that I unfortunately saw when I was ten years old. Although the terror that led me to avert my eyes and hide under my theater seat has long since passed, it amazes me that the images still pop into my mind randomly and uncontrollably. How much more common must that experience be for young people nowadays, who are constantly being bombarded by images from screens of all sizes?

Here parents and teachers face a dilemma about raising and educating teenagers in today's world. On the one hand Steiner exhorts high school teachers to connect young people with the wider world. On the other hand, what if that larger world is largely an artificial construct, a virtual reality? How can we Waldorf teachers make our peace with an electronically dominated media culture? What are our choices? Do we turn into Luddites and try to protect our young charges from the media onslaught, or do we simply surrender, resigning ourselves to the "Hollywoodization" of literature? Awful versions of literary classics abound, from a silly mini-series dramatizing *The Odyssey,* or woefully condensed made-for-television adaptations of *Crime and Punishment* or *Dr. Zhivago*, to distorted movie versions of many of Shakespeare's plays. One of the worst films I have ever seen featured Demi Moore as Hester Prynne in *The Scarlet Letter*, whose producers apparently could not stand the idea of Hester's minister and lover, Arthur Dimmesdale, dying on that fateful scaffold, as author Nathaniel Hawthorne originally wrote. So they actually completely altered Hawthorne's tragic ending; they had Hester and Dimmesdale riding off into the sunset together, presumably without all that awful suffering and guilt and dying that "cluttered up" Hawthorne's version.

How we resolve these questions about the media will have a direct effect upon our teaching of ninth graders. They are, after all, most impressionable and almost fragile in their fledgling capacities. By its very nature, adolescent development bears the stamp of a kind of exile. It is no accident that Steiner used the term "astral body" to refer to the birth of this new, inward consciousness. Surely "astral" suggests a heavenly origin. In a cosmic sense, puberty accentuates the "casting out" from heavenly spheres that earthly birth signifies. Is it any wonder that teenagers express disillusionment in a material world that is but a most imperfect reflection of a spiritual realm? Perhaps the virtual realities found in movies and video games attract young people precisely because they offer an escape from the unpleasantness that they often experience on the physical plane. However, I would urge teachers to not surrender completely to the onslaught of media. As difficult as it is to compete with all the external images that besiege our students today, it is more imperative than ever to offer counter-images of the most potent kind—inner imaginations that will resonate long after the initial, inner picturing.

Building Confidence through Grammar

We also need to anchor our students in the physical world without imprisoning them in a materialistic worldview. Strengthening their powers of observation helps to ground them, and schooling the imagination gives them inner mobility. There is a third capacity we need to foster in ninth graders: confidence—an assurance that the world proceeds according to a kind of lawfulness, and that they can develop the skills to apprehend that lawfulness. In the humanities, grammar can be the perfect vehicle.

Just mentioning the word "grammar" can elicit a collective inner groan from adults who suffered through years of sentence diagramming and endless recitations of seemingly senseless rules. I have never felt the aversion towards grammar that so many of my contemporaries feel. I have always appreciated its certainty, its almost mathematical precision. A predicate adjective always equals its antecedent subject, a participial phrase always modifies a noun, a preposition is always followed by its own object...except, of course, when we hear even the most educated of politicians and news commentators say, "Between you and I, Diane..." when the object becomes an ill-chosen, out-of-place subject.

Why keep struggling against the popular culture's seemingly inexorable disregard for proper grammar? Does it really portend the end of civilization if more and more people are confusing subject and object, or if they have no clue about the agreement needed for singular and plural references? Well, there is the confusion factor; if a *single* person gets into *their* car, and then drives to *their* boyfriend's house for a late-night tryst, how many people will actually show up?

Two compelling reasons prompt us to continue fighting the good grammar fight. On the cultural level, much of George Orwell's prophetic vision about the shriveling of language has come true: the contraction of individual words to the smallest possible monosyllabic pieces—*fax* from facsimile, *dis* from disrespect, laser, and so forth; the interchangeability of verbs and nouns (strategize, prioritize, let's party!); the use of intensifiers (he thought "plus" and "double plus" might do it—we use supersize it, superstar, megahit, ultrasoft); the use of doublespeak to couch actual meanings in an obfuscating haze—"peacekeepers" for lethal missiles, "theater of conflict" for war zones, "pacification of Iraq" and "shock and awe" for mobilizing military might to kill as many of the enemy in as short a time as possible.

We should remember that Orwell's totalitarian vision included a greater end than simply reducing the reservoir of words available to us. The ruling party wanted, as far as possible, to make human speech independent of consciousness. What would such a culture look like? People might mindlessly mouth commercial jingles such as, "Just do it," "This Bud's for you," "Like a rock," "Is it in you?" or "I'm lovin' it." They would rely on clichés and familiar phrasing to express what would pass for thoughts.

> I wish you'd have given me this written question ahead
> of time so I could plan for it. I'm sure something will pop
> into my head here in the midst of this press conference,
> with all the pressure of trying to come up with answer, but

it hadn't yet. I don't want to sound like I have made no mistakes. I'm confident I have. I just haven't—you just put me under the spot here, and maybe I'm not as quick on my feet as I should be in coming up with one. (President George W. Bush, after being asked to name the biggest mistake he had made)[12]

Or,

Our enemies are innovative and resourceful, and so are we. They never stop thinking about new ways to harm our country and our people, and neither do we.[13]

They would, in short, live in a condition of ever-diminishing consciousness about themselves and about the effects of their words. Do we really need to question whether Waldorf education is needed as a force for cultural renewal?

The second reason for defending the grammatical correctness of the English language has again to do with our mission of helping our students incarnate in the healthiest manner possible. The volatile nature of the ninth grader calls for containment, and the order and precision that informs grammar serves that purpose in a way few subjects can. Just as the skeleton provides the hidden scaffolding to articulate the beauty and symmetry of the human form, grammar gives language cohesiveness and reassuring "structural integrity." However, mastering grammar deepens far more than one's capacity for speaking and writing properly. As mysterious as it sounds, Steiner stated clearly on a number of occasions that learning grammar is one of the most vital subjects for the development of the ego. "If language were taught without grammar, man would only attain consciousness, but no consciousness of self. An impossibility. We would not provide man with the inner solidity he needs for life."[14]

If the ego is, on one mundane level, the organizing, integrating principle behind selfhood, then we exercise their fledgling egos by challenging students to discover the lawfulness behind grammatical patterns. The key word here is "discover." I could never understand why teachers believed that merely handing their students the rules and then throwing out a bunch of examples was very engaging. I prefer to begin from the examples and have students discover the rule. Here is an example using dangling modifiers. For each of the sentences below, I ask students to identify a common problem:

- *Earl found an old cabin walking in the woods.*
- *Fatima studied a picture of a rhinoceros reading* National Geographic.
- *Burnt to a crisp, Alberta took the chicken out of the oven.*
- *He suddenly remembered his dead aunt eating his morning bowl of cornflakes.*
- *Snarling and ripping his jeans, Mrs. Tupper tried to protect her husband from the savage pit bull.*
- *The dressy bow on her bosom hanging to the floor was yellow.*

It doesn't take long for the students to see that the phrasing of each sentence has caused unintentional confusion. Once they understand that they do not have to rewrite the whole sentence, but rather only relocate the dangling participial phrase, they can formulate a general rule about such modifiers, such as: "To avoid confusion, place participial phrases next to the words they modify." In this manner, they engage in an active, analytical process of discovery, instead of some rote application of a rule to which they have no real connection.

Despite the joy of discovery, most ninth graders do not possess a natural affinity for learning grammar—unless they see a practical application that makes the exertion worth their while. Since teenagers usually *do* want to express themselves in the most emphatic ways, English teachers would be wise to link the study of grammar to this need for adolescent self-expression, especially by focusing on writing.

In an age where, via instant messaging and e-mailing, young people communicate more through the written word than they ever have—but also more informally—the Word has become increasingly utilitarian, abbreviated, and adulterated. Just as we mentioned the necessity of counteracting the media assault on young people by strengthening our students' own inner, image-creating capacities, so we must also offer a counterpoint to the "dumbing down" of writing. Adolescents need to experience the power, the beauty and the precision of language. One exercise I find helpful in this last regard sharpens both grammatical understanding and writing skills.

Ninth graders tend towards the general rather than the specific in their writing. When asked to depict a woodland scene, they might describe a meadow alive with generic flowers and unidentified birds in undifferentiated trees. Except for including a squirrel or two scampering about, freshmen can be content with broad and nebulous characterizations. I ask such students to divide a piece of paper into three columns, with the words Category, Type and Example at the top of each column. Then I give them a number of nouns to put in the category column, for example, *occupation, instrument, clothing.* In the second column students must identify more narrowly a type of occupation, animal, and so forth, and in the third column, an even more specific example of that type, all the time using only nouns.

Category	*Type*	*Example*
Tree	Evergreen	Cedar
Flower	Perennial	Buttercups
Bird	Redbird	Cardinal
Occupation	Craftsman	Jeweler
Animal	Horse	Stallion
Instrument	Drum	Timpani
Car	Toyota	Prius
Weather	Storm	Typhoon
Weapon	Sword	Scimitar

The aim here is to show students how much more vivid and dynamic their writing can be by choosing the particular nouns found in the third column that evoke distinct images. With apologies to William Carlos Williams, so much depends upon a meadow dappled with buttercups below a cardinal perched in a cedar, beside feather-tailed squirrels.

One other example of incorporating grammatical awareness into a writing exercise is the pattern poem. I put on the board a few, fairly random lines consisting of parts of speech abbreviations, as follows:

> Prep. Phrase
> N. V. Adv.
> Prep. Phrase
> Prep. Phrase

Students then find creative combinations of words to replace the abbreviations:

> Through the murk
> Goldfish cruise unaware
> Of their reflection
> In a cat's eyes.

Little gems can emerge from such exercises. However, the aim here is not necessarily to produce great poetry, but to quicken within the students the idea that learning grammar can help them become more potent, expressive writers.

Teaching the Novel

Compared to other literary genres—epic, lyric, and dramatic—the novel is like the delightful youngest child who combines the best qualities of his or her older siblings. The ancient epic form, with its stately narrative voice, seemed perfectly suited to relating timeless stories on a grand scale, of titanic clashes between larger-than-life heroes and mythical monsters, of gods and mortals, of archetypal journeys over perilous seas. The lyric voice, relying most often upon the short-long, iambic cadences that echo the rhythm of the heart, enabled writers to express the most evocative descriptions and private feelings in the more personal form of the shorter poem. As we have seen in *Oedipus* and *A Raisin in the Sun*, the human relationships portrayed in the dramatic mode provide an intensity and immediacy that can arise only in the dynamic present of the stage. Yet the novel, emerging as an innovative literary form in the West in the seventeenth century, combined the possibilities of its predecessors in exciting new ways (even the root of the word *novel* suggests "newness"). It could combine the narrative perspective and panoramic sweep of the epic, the confessional intimacies of the lyric, and, through dialogue, the complexities of human interaction usually reserved for the theater.

One of the challenges for a teacher is finding the right story to exemplify the best that the novel has to offer. Very few novels at all possess that epic sweep, leavened by lyric passages and dramatic exchanges. Fewer still seem suitable for ninth graders, who usually can't yet apprehend or appreciate cosmic themes or literary acrobatics. So it may seem strange that for years the novel we have chosen for our freshmen has been Herman Melville's masterpiece, *Moby Dick*. Frankly, when teachers at other schools hear this, they think we're kidding. "*Moby Dick* is too large, too complicated, too deep," they say. "Nobody before eleventh or twelfth grade should have to read it. You are a sadistic psychopath if you make your poor ninth graders slog through that tome."

Actually, in many ways *Moby Dick* is the ideal book for freshmen. It contains three ingredients essential for ninth graders. (1) It is first and foremost an adventure story, complete with an archetypal journey away from home into the great unknown. (2) It is filled with compelling characters: the obsessed Captain Ahab; poor, lost, mad Pip; the noble "savage" Queequeg; the shadowy Parsee Fedallah;

Ishmael, Melville's unassuming alter ego and narrator; even the magnificent White Whale itself. (3) Melville balances the book's deeper metaphysical speculations with graphic explanations of the whaling trade. Ninth graders in need of grounding and concreteness in their thinking usually relish the detailed descriptions of how men harvested whale oil using nineteenth century technology.

Each of these aspects of the novel deserves deeper exploration. Who can deny *Moby Dick*'s appeal to adolescents as a tale of adventure? Teenagers seem inherently drawn to danger, to "edges." This is no less true in the literature they read than in the thrills they seek outside of school. In the heart-pounding confrontations with the White Whale during the three days of "The Chase," students experience vicariously the extraordinary risks seamen faced every time they lowered their whaleboats and rowed in hot pursuit of their gigantic prey.

Why do teenagers crave excitement? Perhaps part of the answer can be found in the nature of this newly emerging inner life, the astral body. Prior to puberty, young children are drawn to the reassuring predictability of rhythmic activity. Watch first and second graders at play; they sing rhyming ditties while they hop, skip, jump rope, swing, or bounce balls. They drink in the repetitive motifs of fairy tales, and they will correct you if you tell any sequence involving the archetypal "threeness" out of order.

With the advent of adolescence, however, this innate feeling for rhythm dies away. The appearance of the astral body seems to disrupt natural rhythms. Teenagers' speech patterns suggest lack of inner harmony; instead of the steady, almost musical cadences of younger children, teenagers begin to mumble or shriek in ear-splitting outbursts. For boys, their very gait can become gawky or shambling; for girls their relatively new monthly cycles are often wildly erratic, as are their moods. The production of hormones has an almost intoxicating effect on teenagers, and they begin looking for experiences that will shock and stimulate their newly intensified feeling life. PG-13 movies seem passé; instead they sneak into horror flicks and other R-rated thrillers. They are no longer content with anything that smacks of rhythm or routine. The faculty at the Green Meadow Waldorf School decided long ago to design the weekly schedule for high school so that each day students encounter a different sequence of classes.

In the classes themselves, Waldorf teachers work hard during a lesson to keep students engaged. We know that appealing to only the cerebral side of young people creates a one-sided intellectuality. One of Steiner's most fervent exhortations was to address the *whole* child, in adolescence no less than in early childhood. We want to appeal to students' feelings and will as well as their thinking. Variety seems to be a key here; in any given hour-and-forty-minute lesson, students might be asked to recite a passage from the novel, sing a sea chantey, recall turning points in Melville's biography, engage in a spirited discussion about the positive and negative associations related to Moby Dick's whiteness. Furthermore, they might be encouraged to write a composition imagining themselves as whalers writing in a journal, or to draw an illustration showing the difference between the harpoon and the killing lance, or to learn how to make use of the knots that seamen employ in their daily trade—the overhead, double half-hitch, larkshead, tautline hitch, double fisherman's, and all-important bowline knots. Such varied engagement serves ninth graders particularly well. It sharpens their powers of thinking, but it also arouses their sympathies and—through the discipline of artistic and practical activity—schools their will. Ideally, every class is an adventure, filled with opportunities for risk-taking, challenge, and discovery.

Part of that discovery should involve meeting memorable characters in challenging situations. The captain and crew of the *Pequod* certainly qualify on both counts. When the unlikely partnership of Manhattanite Ishmael and Polynesian Prince Queequeg forms at Peter Coffin's Spouter Inn, and they subsequently board the *Pequod*, they are stepping out of any contemporary teenager's comfortable world, into an unfamiliar realm where the rules of the solid earth no longer seem to apply. In the very first chapter, Melville points to the mystical allure of the water. "Why did the old Persians hold the sea holy? Why did the Greeks give it a separate deity, and make him the own brother of Jove?"[15]

In myths and stories around the globe, a journey across water seems to signify an entrance into an otherworldly, spiritual dimension. The cautionary tales of Noah and Jonah in the Bible come to mind. The Sumerian King Gilgamesh, grieving for his lost companion Enkidu, must cross the Sea of Death in search of the secret to immortal life; he returns to Uruk a transformed man. The Greeks pictured the dead being ferried across the River Styx to the dreary Land of the Shades. As we will examine more closely when we discuss the tenth grade, Homer's Odysseus can only gain the qualities he needs after enduring a decade of trials at sea. Jason and the Argonauts' quest for the Golden Fleece is another voyage with spiritual implications. Shakespeare's Prospero raises a storm in *The Tempest* to bring his enemies to his island. Only after the harrowing shipwreck can they experience a spiritual awakening that their own pangs of conscience (and another's forgiveness) can provide. Coleridge's *Rime of the Ancient Mariner* chronicles the suffering and redemption of a seafaring man who thoughtlessly destroys one of God's creatures. More recently, Hemingway's classic *The Old Man and The Sea* uses this motif to show the old man's transformation in his epic battle with his marlin "brother."

The voyage of the *Pequod* joins the ranks of these archetypal seagoing quests. The *Pequod*'s crew comprises an isolated, floating universe. Even high school freshmen can see how the ship, with its motley assortment of international characters, becomes a rather thinly veiled metaphor for the macrocosm of the earth, spinning through the immensity of the larger universe. Their voyage becomes all of humanity's. In Ahab's intensity, Starbuck's civility, Flask's bravado, students can see aspects of themselves. Melville hints at this mirroring quality in the very first chapter when he refers to the myth of Narcissus,

> who because he could not grasp the tormenting, mild image he saw in the fountain, plunged into it and was drowned. But that same image, we ourselves see in all rivers and oceans. It is the image of the ungraspable phantom of life; and this is the key to it all.[16]

No character seems to reflect Narcissus' plight as much as the tormented, larger-than-life figure of Captain Ahab. In Ahab ninth graders meet a man who looks into the depths of the ocean and sees in Moby Dick

> the monomaniac incarnation of all those malicious agencies which some deep men feel eating in them, till they are left living with half a heart and half a lung. That intangible malignity which has been from the beginning. All the subtle demonisms of life and thought, all evil, to crazy Ahab, were visibly personified and made practically assailable in Moby Dick. He piled upon the whale's white hump the sum of all the general rage and hate felt by his whole race from Adam down.[17]

Ahab's fixation on the White Whale often leads ninth graders to fruitful discussions about the nature of obsession. They see that for all of Ahab's "infinity of firmest fortitude, a determinate, unsurrenderable willfulness," he has been enslaved by his obsession. In one class we had a lively discussion about how obsession was akin to addiction. Students identified different levels of addiction, from the seemingly harmless ones such as being a "chocoholic" or video game maniac to more serious addictions such as gambling or substance abuse. It seemed fortuitous that these young people, on the verge of encountering one or another of the adult world's many temptations, could recognize in Melville's characters the consequences of succumbing to one's uncontrollable passions or desires.

The third ingredient that makes Moby Dick a desirable novel for ninth graders is often overlooked by modern readers: the extensive, fascinating process of extracting oil from the whale. Melville depicts in graphic detail the actual whale chase—the harpooner's hurling of the barbed iron and the ensuing "Nantucket sleigh ride" whereby the whale can drag a whaleboat for miles before tiring enough for the whale men to pull in the line. He recounts how, when the boat has been maneuvered alongside the exhausted prey, the boat steersman plunges the killing lance deep into whale, churning and churning the tip until he pierces the whale's heart. The students react with a mixture of repugnance and awe as Melville describes the whale's final flurry. In agony and terror as it spouts its own clotted blood, it can swamp the whaleboat with its last, violent flailing and lashing of its tail.

The intent in reading these episodes is not to sensationalize the brutal killing of the whales, although the revulsion many students feel can itself be an awakening experience for young people unaware of exploitative fishing practices that continue into the present day. In fact, the process of harvesting the whale oil can be an instructive one for ninth graders needing to bring a certain rational sequencing into their thought life. They follow the "cutting in" of the "blanket," or layer of blubber, once the whale has been towed back to the mother ship. They draw illustrations of the blubbery mass being hoisted via block and tackle above the deck of the ship, then lowered into the blubber room where it is cut into smaller sections called "horse pieces," and further sliced into "bible leaves," like the pages of a book. From there it goes back up to the tryworks, or brick furnaces, on the main deck and thrown into huge, heated pots, until the fat is rendered into oil and poured off into casks and stored in the hold below. Students learn that one of the great ironies of the whole oil-producing process involves the "fritters" or "cracklings"—that shriveled, crispened blubber residue left behind after the oil has been extracted—that are used to feed the very flames that burn future blubber. Thus "the whale supplies his own fuel and burns by his own body."[18]

Melville sees metaphors everywhere. Even in the utilitarian tryworks he draws parallels to Ahab.

> As their uncivilized laughter forked upwards out of them, like the flames from the furnace...as the wind howled on, and the sea leaped, and the ship groaned and dived, and yet steadfastly shot her red hell further and further into the blackness of the sea and the night...then the rushing *Pequod*, freighted with savages, and laden with fire, and burning a corpse, and plunging into that blackness of darkness, seemed the material counterpart of her monomaniac commander's soul.[19]

So the technical description of whaling really becomes inseparable from the rich characterizations that carry the story. The powerful imagery needs little commentary at the ninth grade level; students are usually content to understand the literal meaning and to have only an inkling of deeper meanings. Yet occasionally Melville provides the students with a metaphor that is immediately accessible to them. In another scene during the "cutting in" sequence, Queequeg is balancing on the whale corpse's slippery back to cut a hole for the blubber hook. Ishmael stands on the deck and protects his friend below from falling into the ocean by means of a "monkey rope" attached to both men's waists. However, Ishmael realizes the precarious nature of both men's situations:

> For better or for worse, we two, for the time, were wedded; and should poor Queequeg sink to rise no more, then both usage and honor demanded, that instead of cutting the

cord, it should drag me down in his wake. ... I saw that this situation of mine was the precise situation of every mortal that breathes. ...If your banker breaks, you snap; if your apothecary by mistake sends you poison in your pills, you die.[20]

In underscoring the interdependence of all people, Melville is speaking to the ideal of brotherhood and sisterhood that lives so deeply in these young people. One of the true benefits of the advent of the internet and the cell phone is the increasing sense of our connectivity to people around the world. This growing global consciousness was seen in the overwhelming outpouring support for relief efforts in the aftermath of a number of recent natural disasters—the tsunami in Southeast Asia, Hurricane Katrina, the earthquake in Pakistan. In several of his writings, Rudolf Steiner foresaw that there would come a day when well-fed people would be unable to sleep at night as long as there were children going to bed hungry somewhere in the world. "In the future no human being is to find peace in the enjoyment of happiness if others beside him are unhappy.[21] The proliferation of organizations created to end hunger, to educate the disadvantaged, to fight the ravages of AIDs, and to take in orphans from war-torn lands testifies to this growing identification of privileged people with the oppressed and suffering.

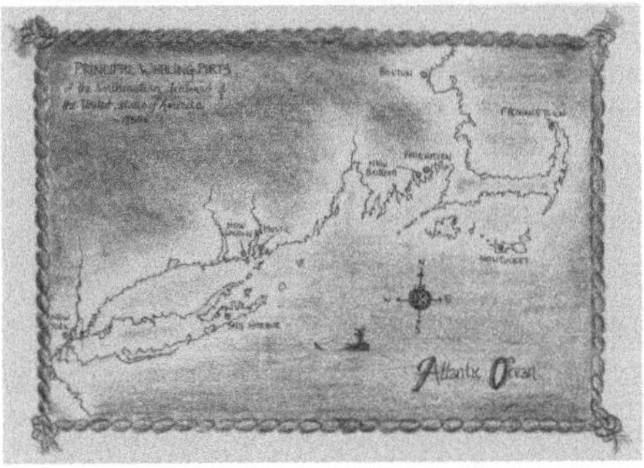

Figure 1 – Classwork during Moby Dick *main lesson*

Figure 2 – Classwork during Moby Dick *main lesson*

Other Ninth Grade Readings

Over the years we have introduced ninth graders to a variety of other novels, with varying degrees of success. Carson McCullers' *The Heart Is a Lonely Hunter* seemed like a suitable choice for a while, but the suicide of the mute at the end left too many students unsettled and crestfallen. The same could be said of Steinbeck's *Of Mice and Men*; Lennie's "merciful" killing of George had a disheartening effect on a number of freshmen. I am not suggesting that one should protect ninth graders from books with unhappy endings. After all, what story ends as excruciatingly as *Oedipus Rex* or as heartbreakingly as *Romeo and Juliet*? Indeed, teenagers around this age begin to crave some "darkness" in their lives, a kind of "soul pain" that confirms their ability to increasingly experience the world's woe as sharply as their own. If they can find it vicariously in the books they read, instead of embracing this darkness in their real lives, all the better.

However, teachers need to be careful not to pander to this adolescent hunger for the disturbing or shocking. There are plenty of books that leave the reader devastated by the end, without any sense of hope or redemption; Huxley's *Brave New World* and Orwell's *1984* both come to mind. We have tried to stay away from such literature for freshmen, who are more impressionable and sensitive than they would ever admit. Instead, we have looked for stories that contain both the sorrows and the joys of human experience, the despair as well as the faith that can help to heal the despairing. One timeless novel that has met these requirements year after year is Alan Paton's *Cry, the Beloved Country*. Written in the middle of the last century and set in South Africa, Paton tells the story of two fathers—one white, one native—both of whom lose their sons in a tragic, violent encounter, and who then devote their lives to undoing some of the worst damage engendered by the rampant racism of the time. Even though apartheid is now, thankfully, no longer the official policy of the South African government, students can still recognize in that country, and perhaps even in their own, the residue of racial bigotry that arises from ignorance and the measures needed to combat such prejudice.

Another twentieth century novel that is often the first book we have ninth graders read in the fall is Forrest Carter's *The Education of Little Tree*. The story of an orphan taken in by his Cherokee grandparents who live close to the land in the backwoods of the Smoky Mountains, *Little Tree* combines humor, pathos and chapter after chapter of life lessons for students. In an early chapter entitled "The Secret Place," Little Tree finds some sweet-smelling musk bugs and shares his new-found knowledge with his Granma, who can hardly contain her excitement at discovering this scent, and who then tells Granpa.

> Granpa was struck dumfounded. I let him smell of them and he said he had lived seventy odd years, total unaware of such a smell.
> Granma said I had done right, for when you come on something that is good, first thing to do is share it with whoever you can find; that way, the good spread out to where no telling it will go. Which is right.[22]

In another episode, Granpa takes Little Tree out to witness how the local fox outsmarts Granpa's hounds.

> Granpa said the reason ol' Slick had waited so long for the hounds to get close is that he wanted his scent to be fresh on the rocks, figuring that the hounds' *feelings* would take over from their *sense*, when they got excited. It worked too, with ol' Rippitt and Bess. ...
> Granpa said he had many's the time seen that same kind of thing, feelings taking over sense, make as big a fools out of people as it had ol' Rippitt. Which I reckin is so.[23]

Such explicit, folksy lessons speak so accessibly to contemporary youth as to make comments from the teacher an unnecessary intrusion.

Some teachers have shied away from the book because of the controversy kicked up by research into Forrest Carter's past, which points to the author's involvement earlier in his life as a member of the Ku Klux Klan and the speechwriter for George Wallace responsible for Wallace's infamous campaign slogan: "Segregation today! Segregation tomorrow! Segregation forever!" Carter's repugnant political views contrast so sharply with the sensitive portrayals in *The Education of Little Tree* that the question must be raised about the significance of an author's real-life beliefs. Is the book cleverly disguised, manipulative pap designed to dupe sentimental, New Age liberals, or is it a universal story extolling the virtues of tolerance and courage, self-reliance and reverence for nature? Was Carter a charlatan or a transformed man towards the end of his life? Can light really emanate out of such darkness?

I side with Dee Brown, author of the brilliant 1970 work *Bury My Heart at Wounded Knee,* which chronicles the systematic genocide of America's native peoples by the dominant white culture and which obliterated forever the stereotype of the Native American "savage." Brown said, "If people like the book, what does it matter who the author is?"[24] While it might be instructive to discuss the author's views *after* students read such a book, it makes little sense to boycott the book, or to bias young readers by alerting them to the controversy *before* they read *Little Tree.* How many great works have been created by artists with unsavory pasts or objectionable values?

A final word should be added about two other popular books that seem perfectly pitched for ninth graders. One is Harper Lee's *To Kill a Mockingbird,* and the other is *The Diary of Anne Frank.* Clearly young people, who are aflame with passion to redress all the injustice and suffering in the world but who can also be victims of their own narrow-minded and critical natures, need examples of living idealism to emulate. In *Mockingbird*, Atticus Finch's decision to defend an innocent black man accused of raping a white girl exemplifies an unshakable moral uprightness and conviction in the face of deep-rooted intolerance. The book is filled with acts of kindness and of courage, none more surprising than Boo Radley's rescue of Jem and Scout when they are attacked by the girl's vengeful father towards the end of the story. Boo's emergence, from being perceived as the town's most mysterious and feared "ghost" to unassuming, heroic neighbor is, in itself, a lesson in the perils of prejudging people.

Reading excerpts from Anne Frank's diary with ninth graders works on a number of levels. It introduces them to the rewards that writing in a daily journal can provide. It connects students with historical conditions so monstrous that they would be unimaginable without the humanizing perspective Anne brings to her years in the secret annex. No matter how burdened modern American teenagers perceive their lives to be, they inevitably feel their troubles pale beside Anne's tribulations. Yet they recognize Anne as one of them. She writes with such an accessible blend of adolescent longing, all-too-familiar self-absorption, and irrepressible love for the possibilities life might have to offer. "If God lets me live, I shall attain more than Mummy ever has done. I shall not remain insignificant; I shall work in the world and for mankind!"[25]

At the same time, Anne's insights into her own character and into the people closest to her bear the mark of an "old soul." "I have an odd way of sometimes, as it were, being able to see myself through someone else's eyes. Then I view the affairs of a certain 'Anne' at my ease, and browse through the pages of her life as if she were a stranger."[26] These extraordinary moments of clarity and detachment exemplify the objectivity that teachers wish for every ninth grader. Anne even suggests a kind of meditative approach, familiar to students of Rudolf Steiner's anthroposophy, which can help develop this quality.

How noble and good everyone could be if, every evening before falling asleep, they were to recall to their minds the events of the whole day and consider exactly what has been good and bad. Then, without realizing it, you try to improve yourself at the start of each new day.[27]

Ultimately, Anne speaks to young people as a guiding angel might, reminding them of their own better selves. She manages to stay true to her vision of the higher, to those ideals that can buoy teenagers up in what can become increasingly choppy waters.

I am young and I possess many buried qualities; I am young and strong and am living a great adventure; I am still in the midst of it and can't grumble the whole day long. I have been given a lot, a happy nature, a great deal of cheerfulness and strength. Every day I feel that I am developing inwardly, that the liberation is drawing nearer and how beautiful nature is, how good the people are about me, how interesting this adventure is! Why, then, should I be in despair?[28]

Tenth Grade:
Logic and Lawfulness

The Oddest Sea: Teaching *The Odyssey*

It may sound like hyperbole to speak about a dramatic change that occurs in sophomores. Yet those teachers who deal with adolescents day-to-day and month-to-month will attest to the surprising transformation that can occur in the summer between the ninth and tenth grade years. Perhaps it has something to do with having a year of high school already under their belts, or perhaps it can be attributed to natural maturation; in either case, sophomores often return to school in the autumn much fuller of themselves than they were as humbler ninth graders. Instead of seeing them flailing about in the aforementioned ninth grade swamp, we might picture them as the self-assured crew members of a sleek, Greek sailing ship, leaving the protective home harbor, setting out for open water. They seem more comfortable with themselves, conceptually clearer, and more confident than ever of their cognitive abilities.

Yet over the years we teachers have noticed another pattern that often emerges during tenth grade. Perhaps it can be traced to this newfound confidence that can border on brazenness. Whatever the reason, many sophomores will go "overboard." Sometime during the year they will get themselves in some kind of trouble—with drugs, sex, stealing, lying. In other words, many tenth graders succumb at one point or another during the year to those myriad temptations the world has to offer. Is this true for all sophomores? Of course not; some dismayed parents discover that their sons or daughters "fall" in sixth or seventh grade, some not until much later, some not at all, but here I am referring to a general tendency whose "rightful" time frame, you might say, occurs sometime in students' sophomore year.

This tendency to fall prey to such temptations is one of the reasons why we introduce our tenth graders to Homer's *The Odyssey*. Now what can twenty-first century teenagers—for whom life before cell phones is but a dim memory—really learn from a nearly three-thousand-year-old epic journey? If, as has already been suggested, the Waldorf school curriculum both reflects and addresses the needs of the developing child, in the high school no less than at the nursery/ kindergarten or elementary school levels, then what possible adolescent need can be met by transporting tenth graders back into an ancient story teeming with mythological instead of technological marvels—man-eating monsters, ship-swallowing whirlpools, raging sea-gods, and lethal enchantresses?

The Odyssey has always been a staple of high school classrooms. Generations of students have studied this sequel to the Trojan War as a window into Homeric Greece, as a Jungian banquet of archetypal psychological motifs, as a classic tale of loss, longing and reunion. It has gracefully borne all these interpretations and many others, but at its core, *The Odyssey* depicts the birth pangs of a new stage in human development.

We can recognize in Odysseus the strivings of not only a single human being, but also of an entire age. As a representative of humanity, he presages the dawning of a vital emerging culture, founded upon a new rationality and investigative spirit that would culminate in the Golden Age of Greece. As an individual, Odysseus embodies the first stirrings of an intellectually vigorous, ego-directed self. For tenth graders awakening to their own fledgling intellectual capacities, and often intoxicated with the power of their incipient egos, Odysseus' face is a familiar reflection in the literary mirror.

It should be noted that *The Odyssey* seems far more appropriate for sophomores than *The Iliad* does, whose central character is Achilles. Considered by many to be the noblest Greek warrior of them all, Achilles has much more in common with freshmen than Odysseus does. Achilles is peerless in battle; only a single, vulnerable heel keeps him from being one of the Immortals. Yet his pouting over the loss of a female "trophy" is the real focus of *The Iliad*. For all of his prowess in combat, Achilles is in the thrall of his own emotions, veering from envy to loathing and from grief to rage. This final fury boils up in him as he discovers that his best friend has been slain in battle after donning Achilles' armor. Although Achilles avenges his friend's death by killing the great Trojan hero Hector, he only hastens his own demise. From the ramparts of Troy, Hector's brother Paris shoots the arrow that pierces Achilles' mortal heel.

Ultimately, Achilles' plight has little more to teach adolescents than to serve as a cautionary tale. They see his petulance for what it is—the childish display of a man who has little control over his impulses. His story lacks an ingredient essential to virtually all of the literature we choose to explore with high school students—the possibility of self-transformation, or at least of self-knowledge. Blinded by emotional outbursts and unenlightened by a slumbering intellect, Achilles represents an outmoded form of consciousness (albeit one that stubbornly persists into this century) that perpetuates, and then falls victim to, a seemingly endless cycle of vengeance and violence.

Wily Odysseus is a more modern and complex character, whose craftiness really appeals to tenth graders' own sharpening intellects. He gives them a metaphorical reflection of their own struggles to master themselves as they encounter the world's many enticements, which brings us back to a primary reason for introducing this epic to sophomores. On a fundamental level Homer's epic is a story about how a man and his crew deal with one temptation after another.

When Odysseus triumphantly sets out from Troy, he has every reason to believe that he will soon be back in his native Ithaka, holding his beloved wife Penelope and young son Telemakhos in his arms. After all, it was his brilliant idea to construct the gift of the wooden horse that led to the Greeks' final victory. In addition, he has become Athena's favorite mortal, so enamored is she of his "bottomless bag of tricks." Surely a man with such cunning could surmount any obstacles on his return voyage. Yet along the way

Odysseus encounters twelve perils that reveal his weaknesses and test his reserves of guile, endurance and resistance to temptation. Like Hercules' twelve labors, these challenges act as crucibles that both cause Odysseus enormous suffering and define his greatness. Ultimately, the anguish he undergoes transforms and ennobles Odysseus, making him worthy of reuniting with the pure-hearted Penelope.

Throughout his journey home, Odysseus must grapple with the same archetypal temptations that entrap today's adolescents. He must overcome Circe the sorceress, who appears to satisfy a man's every desire, just before transforming him into a pig. Even after he rescues his men from their animal state, Odysseus falls prey to Circe's potent charms. He shares her "flawless bed" for almost a year before he realizes that her enchantments have diverted him from returning to his true soul mate.

On another island, Odysseus must wrest his men away from the Lotus Eaters, who offer his crew members the promise of days passed in a dreamy, narcotic stupor. Still later, he manages to save his men from the Sirens, those irresistible nymphs whose music is so overpowering that sailors will wreck their ships on the jagged rocks just to get closer to the source of that music.

When these tenth graders realize that they are not the first to discover the risky allure of "sex, drugs, and rock 'n roll," they get very interested in how Odysseus copes with all these temptations. And they see a man who is much like them; he has greatness within him and a burning desire to test his mettle, but he also struggles with lack of self-restraint, lack of humility. These two soul powers are just what he needs to develop if he is to win his way back home.

Early on his return voyage, Odysseus and his crew find themselves in the land of the Cyclops, probably the best-known of their adventures. Their predicament (finding themselves trapped in Polyphemus the Cyclops' cave) and Odysseus' crafty breakout plan after blinding the giant (avoiding detection by clutching the underbellies of the sheep as they exit the cave) are well-known to *Odyssey*-lovers. Fewer readers recall Odysseus' exceedingly poor judgment and display of arrogance at a critical moment during his crew's escape. After he has already secured his anonymity by cannily telling Polyphemus that his name is "Nobody," the impetuous side of Odysseus takes over. He simply cannot refrain from crowing about his own cleverness. From the deck of his departing ship, Odysseus shouts back to the blinded giant,

> Cyclops, if ever mortal man inquire
> how you were put to shame and blinded, tell him
> Odysseus, raider of cities, took your eye.[29]

Perhaps more than at any other moment in the story, tenth graders recognize in Odysseus their own hubris, their own lack of self-restraint. Just as Odysseus' egotistical indiscretion causes the sea-god Poseidon, father of Polyphemus, to raise a ship-shattering tempest that delays Odysseus' homecoming by a decade, so adolescent impetuosity can cause "shipwrecks" whenever such rashness erupts. Yet for all the damage they can inflict, experiences fraught with such thoughtlessness can also furnish young people with opportunities for what the Greeks termed *anagnorisis*—the self-recognition that can lead to individual growth.

It takes a decade of ordeals for Odysseus to achieve some measure of mastery over himself. Winning one's way to selfhood rarely comes without a stiff price. At the beginning of his voyage home Odysseus possesses all the trappings worthy of the king of Ithaka—ships laden with the spoils of war, a reputation for valor and cunning, a proud crew, a magnificent queen. By the time he drags himself to the shore of yet another strange island, he has lost nearly everything—his ships, the spoils, his entire crew, even his apparel. Naked, shivering, half-drowned, Odysseus has nothing he can call his own now except the inextinguishable image of Penelope and whatever inner resources he can summon to face the next trial.

Once again, sophomores can relate to Odysseus' plight. As they teeter between the stages of childhood and adulthood, they have already experienced the dropping away of certain "gifts" that the kingdom of childhood bestowed upon them—the feeling of oneness with their surroundings, the rich and fertile imagination that led to endless hours of play, the obliviousness to the passing of time, the liberating lack of self-consciousness. The waning of these natural attributes leaves teenagers feeling as abandoned and as vulnerable as Odysseus does when he awakens in a remote cove of his native land.

> What am I in for now?
> Whose country have I come to this time?
> Where shall I take...myself,
> With no guide, no directions?...And then he wept
> Despairing, for his own land, trudging down
> Beside the endless wash of the wide, wide sea,
> Weary and desolate as the sea.[30]

Yet this stage of adolescence is absolutely essential if, like Odysseus, teenagers are to complete the voyage "home," that is, to find their way to healthy selfhood. They must leave behind those childhood glories and, largely on their own, forge new capacities that will help them confront the world's challenges as well as tame their own inner storms. At the same time, Homer reminds us that during their most despairing moments, young people need a constant, guiding presence, a vision of their own purer, higher selves—their own steadfast Penelope. She waits with outstretched arms for the Odysseus in every wayfaring individual. Her welcoming embrace serves both as inspiration during the long and arduous journey and as priceless treasure at the journey's end.

The Art of Poetry:
Developing Imagination, Inspiration, and Intuition

Poetry can be taught at any level, of course, but the formal introduction of poetic forms and devices seems particularly suitable for tenth graders. After all, tenth graders are no longer content to answer the "What" question so often posed to their freshmen classmates. Sophomores appear increasingly interested in questions of "How," especially in questions that involve form and structure, logic and lawfulness. They want to know not only what a poem is about, but how the poet creates mood, uses sounds, achieves his or her end. In a course entitled the Art of Poetry in some schools, the Flowering of the English Language in others, students begin to learn the craft of poetry by examining the structural elements of classical and modern poems and then by composing their own creative pieces.

We usually divide this block into three parts. After tracing the fascinating development of the English language out of the cross-pollination that took place among the Anglo-Saxon, Latin and Norman streams, we usually spend several days looking at the Poet as Painter—that is, we look at image-making elements and strive to educate our young poets' outer and inner eyes. They read William Carlos Williams' famous, imagistic poem "The Red Wheelbarrow."

> so much depends
> upon
>
> a red wheel
> barrow
>
> glazed with rain
> water
>
> beside the white
> chickens.[31]

At first, of course, they will wonder about all the fuss over such a seemingly simple poem. Then they will look more attentively at the structure of the piece—at the stark contrast of the red and white, the vividness of the startlingly still, and yet somehow dynamic, scene, perhaps even at the top-heavy, two-line stanzas that visually evoke the shape of a wheelbarrow. Finally, they will wrestle with just what it is that depends so much upon such an everyday scene. Then they find some commonplace, even ugly, object—a piece of broken glass, a rusty nail, a watermelon rind—that they must now describe in the manner of Williams, in other words, with the intention of letting the images speak as purely as possible, without imputing any deeper meaning to them. In another exercise, sophomores choose a photograph or painting to write a poem about; in still another, they select some inanimate object to personify, by giving voice to a teapot or a hand mirror or a bridge. This schooling of observation and imagination is not to be confused with fantasy or some whimsy. The faculty of imagination does not constitute an escape from reality; rather it can plumb a deeper reality, one grounded in the material world but stretching towards, and sometimes even touching, a higher realm.

Another week we consider the Poet as Musician—that is, we study the rhythms, meters, sound devices that poets use to distinguish poetry from prose. Once again we return to the three archetypal literary forms, now as examples of the primary poetic meters: to the epic with its stately, long-short-short, dactylic hexameter, such as in Homer's opening lines from *The Iliad* (*Andra moi enepe musa, polutropon hos mala polla*), to the more intimate lyric's iambic short-long, short-long that echoes the constant drumming of the heart, and to the flexible dramatic genre that intermingles the above meters with the steady, long-short trochaic, the breathless, short-short-long anapest, and the equally stressed spondees to create the natural rhythms found in dialogue.

We explore the music inherent in words by having students taste sounds, first by uttering only vowels, then by pronouncing individual consonants. The exercise brings to their consciousness the two fundamentally distinctive types of sounds. Sophomores discover why vowels are often associated with archetypal soul states: the "aaaaah" that is voiced when we experience some awe-inspiring sight, the "oh" that can result from a moment of surprise, the "ooh" that can express disgust or fear. Vowels ride freely on the stream of our breath, their individual character depending only upon the shape of our mouth. Most consonants (excluding *h* and possibly *w*) arise out of conflict, so to speak, out of the friction that occurs when throat, tongue, teeth or lips interrupt that flow of breath. Students can see right away how the articulation of consonants requires more exertion than the expression of vowels. Together, vowels impart a kind of soul substance to words, while consonants confer the concreteness and vividness that carving or sculpting might provide.

The next step is to have students consider the inherent qualities of sounds. We ask them, "Which sound is quicker—*f* or *b*? Which is heavier—*s* or *d*? Which is harder—*k* or *l*? Was it some random stroke of fortune that led to a dense, rectangular object being called a "brick," while a soft, feathery cushion would be termed a "pillow"? These questions lead naturally to an examination of alliteration, assonance and onomatopoeia and to their effects in poems. Gwendolyn Brooks' short masterpiece is a student favorite.

We Real Cool
The Pool Players.
Seven at the Golden Shovel.

We real cool. We
Left school. We

Lurk late. We
Strike Straight. We

Sing sin. We
Thin gin. We

Jazz June. We
Die soon.[32]

It doesn't take tenth graders long to see how the sounds of this piece create a web that links line to line; how the "l"s of "cool" and "left school" are immediately picked up by the "l"s in the next stanza, how the "s"s of "strike straight" are echoed in "sing sin." The assonance of that short "i," repeated in four words of the third stanza, becomes a phonetic intensive; its very sound suggests an associated feeling of smallness or inconsequentiality; words such as *inch, splinter, cricket, sliver, bit, tic, pill,* and *blip* share this quality. But throughout the poem, the insistent "We" is like an inescapable drum beat, connecting the idea of "ganghood" with that of abrupt and shocking termination at the end of every line, except, of course, the last line, by which time the reader needs no recurring line breaks to underscore Brooks' intent. Through such close reading and "appreciating" of the poet's craft, sophomores begin to attune their ears to the music of the word and of the world. This is a capacity that Rudolf Steiner called inspiration, a kind of "breathing in," a higher knowing through a heightened hearing.

During the final week of the Art of Poetry, we often focus on the Poet as Priest—that is, how poetry can rekindle a kind of reverence in us for the things of this world, seen and unseen. Wendell Berry's lovely poem, "The Wild Geese," captures some of this sense of wonder.

The Wild Geese

Horseback on Sunday morning,
harvest over, we taste persimmon
and wild grape, sharp sweet
of summer's end. In time's maze
over the fall fields, we name names
that went west from here, names
that rest on graves. We open
a persimmon seed to find the tree
that stands in promise,

> pale, in the seed's marrow.
> Geese appear high over us,
> pass, and the sky closes. Abandon,
> as in love or sleep, holds
> them to their way, clear,
> in the ancient faith: what we need
> is here. And we pray, not
> for new earth or heaven, but to be
> quiet in heart, and in eye
> clear. What we need is here.[33]

Berry uses his spare and elegant language to express sentiments that young people inwardly yearn, and need, to hear: the quiet aliveness of and attention to the moment, the season, the senses; the awareness that this moment stands in the grand stream of time, has been built upon the countless lives lived before this one; the possibility of a future as bursting with promise as this present instant; and finally, the absolute appreciation of the here and now. One could choose dozens of other poems that convey this recognition of life's blessings, and that also become transparent enough for students to identify the technique beneath the lines.

Sometimes, as a corollary to this theme, we also address the idea of the Poet as Seer, who intuitively apprehends truths beyond the reach of everyday consciousness. Basho, the seventeenth century Japanese master of haiku, described this intuitive act best. "Poetry issues of its own accord when you and the object have become one, when you have plunged deep enough into the object to see something like a hidden glimmering there." (Burleson)

During each week of this Art of Poetry course students are working on developing their incipient capacities of imagination, inspiration and intuition, even as they focus on learning the poet's craft. These capacities can work in surprisingly subtle and profound ways. Back in 1986, a young man at Green Meadow wrote the following short poem during this course:

The Boy and the Dove

With the morning sun comes the dove,
Her white wings glistening yellow and gold,
She rests herself on a branch of the lone tree.
Across the cold lot comes the boy,
His black boots scraping the black tar;
He reaches the tree and stops.
The world is quiet and the boy gazes at the dove.
The dove transfixes the boy
And the boy is unable to go on.
As the dove flies from the tree,
His curling lips rise.[34]

– Shadrach Woods '88

Six years later, during his senior year at Bowdoin College, at age 21, Shadrach was involved in a skiing accident in Vermont when he lost control and collided with a tree; he died instantly. When one re-reads the poem, now aware of Shadrach's fate, the piece becomes less a potent poem than an almost eerily prescient premonition. It is the most dramatic example I have ever encountered of poetry becoming windows, not only into young people's souls, but into their destinies.

We who live and work with teenagers need to be ever mindful of the revelatory possibilities of poetry, as well as all the other often hidden gifts young people carry within them. We, too, need to cultivate our faculties of imagination, inspiration and intuition—imagination to see not only what our teenagers are at any particular moment, but what they are becoming; inspiration to not only listen to what they say, but to hear beneath the criticizing and complaining to their innermost, unexpressed longings; and intuition to bridge the gulf between us and them, to align ourselves with their sufferings and strivings so that we might truly experience, in Basho's words, their "hidden glimmerings."

Student Poetry:
Windows into the Teenage Soul

In describing the terrain of adolescence, one cannot overlook the teenagers themselves as "primary sources" of revelation. They are, however, by their very nature, usually hard to "read." They develop extraordinarily effective techniques for hiding themselves behind an array of false fronts, evasive maneuvers, and deep freezes. Why do they retreat? Partly for protection, no doubt, because most adolescents go through a phase in which they believe that nobody understands or appreciates who they really are. The truth is that we teachers and parents who have raised these young people generally *do not* understand or appreciate who they are becoming. How can we when, almost daily, they are metamorphosing into young people further and further removed from the children we have adored? How can we when they hide themselves away from us, intuitively knowing as they do that they are at a most delicate stage of the creative process? And the irony of this withdrawal, of course, is that teenagers desperately want to unmask themselves before the world, if only they could be assured the world would be tender in its response.

Hence, a great opportunity arises through writing, and poetry in particular, both for adolescents to find their voices and for us to listen attentively. The German philosopher Jacob Boehme once wrote, "Whatever the self describes, describes the self." As Shadrach Woods' poem demonstrates, nearly always—consciously or not—young people tend to write about themselves. Even more revealing, teenagers' poetry often sheds light on the sometimes elusive, subtle developmental stages they undergo. I have touched on some of the characteristics of the ninth grader in contrast to the tenth grader, but two writing samples may deepen our understanding.

Here is a telling example by a ninth grader, written as an assignment in conjunction with *The Education of Little Tree*. In the chapter "The Secret Place" I alluded to earlier, Little Tree finds a hidden spot, a small enclosure near a stream, surrounded by sweet gum and fern, where he could go to whenever he needed to feel the consolation of surrounding nature or to simply be by himself. So I asked the students to describe a secret place of their own.

Eric's Secret Place

I found it on a biting cold raw fall day. It was beyond the field where we stole the apples in the fall, and over several stone walls and barbed wire fences. It had everything that I was drawn to—tall, grand and dark pine trees, a small pond with a duck family, tall stiff cattails, and a thicket of brambles encircling its edge. The first time I saw it I was young, and I had not been there for a long time since. On a chilled day, cloudy and windy, I returned there to the secret place, amidst the tall pines, the wind ravaging and tearing at them. It was so different from the way I remembered it. On this day it was so barren, cold, and dead. No ducks, no nothing. With the darkened clouds making ominous shapes above me, I returned home like a small child who had just lost his bosom friend. That night I sat a long time, remorseful and saddened, now that the secret place, my secret place, had lost its magic.[35]

– Eric Shurtleff   '96

What's the difference between the two visits? What dramatic change can we recognize? Each time the weather is harsh—biting, cold, raw. The same pond is there, surrounded by the same pine trees. Except for the disappearance of the ducks, what has changed is less the outer world than the boy's inner experience of it all, and that experience is one of almost inexpressible loss. What's been lost? Perhaps the answer becomes clearer in this poem by a tenth grade girl.

Hatching

Her splintered world lies in shards around her;
The warm dark sphere where nothing has a name
Has crumbled and she wakes to cold and pain.
Freedom, fear, confusion, all have found her,
In one great sudden rush they try to drown her.
Her life-blood rushes madly through her veins,
Her naked half-formed fragile, ugly frame
No longer has the sheltering walls that bound her.
She struggles to stand on delicate, unformed feet,
To focus on some distant lights—the Angel's eyes;
They look so quiet, calm, clear-minded, sweet;
She reaches her fingers towards the sky.
Gently her new heart begins to beat;
She spreads her airy wings, begins to fly.[36]
– Frances Pharr '98

    What does this poem share with the first piece? We have another vivid portrait of initial loss and the accompanying pain. This poem also makes reference to a kind of shelter that has been destroyed, and the resulting mood of uncertainty and vulnerability. What better description of this acute teenage awakening to a new condition arising within them, one that over and over again in their poetry is likened to a death. Surely it must be the death of childhood alluded to in the first chapter that they are mourning, that time of innocence with its sheltering and comforting embrace, that timeless time when the world was alive with animals that could speak and with angels that watched over them.

    Perhaps surprisingly, "The Hatching" contains a reference to an angel, and this constitutes a radical departure from the ninth grader's secret place piece. The angel's appearance heralds a dramatic change in the direction and atmosphere of the poem.

The hatching does not end in darkness and despair—rather, on a note of hopefulness, of new life, of expansiveness. "She spreads her airy wings, begins to fly." This last poem may point to a typical developmental step between ninth and tenth graders. The ninth grade boy experienced a grievous loss, but he only seemed dimly aware of the causes; he did not have the perspective to offer a counter-image promising a brighter tomorrow. The tenth grade poet of "Hatching" conveys a profound polarity—not only a kind of death, but a birth as well.

If we are awake to such developments, Waldorf teachers will design a curriculum that both anticipates and strengthens these inner changes. Some sophomores really begin to sense new possibilities; they are eager to exercise this burgeoning capacity of seeing the larger rather than the narrower view. Another literary offering in the tenth grade challenges students to expand their vision to the very limits of time by considering the vast panorama of humanity's story—the Bible.

The Bible as Source of Literature:
From Love of the Law to the Law of Love

Outside of Sunday school, tackling the Bible is always risky. No more controversial book exists; Dan Brown's recent, fictional bestseller *The Da Vinci Code* kicked up a furor in the Catholic Church, but the reactions were lightweight beside the passions aroused whenever the authenticity of the Bible surfaces as a topic of conversation. Just mentioning the Bible seems to split the world into believers and non-believers. For hardliners on both sides, the Bible is either The Way, The Truth, The Word of God, or it is a collection of myths and inventions, diverting at best, dangerously misleading and divisive at worst.

Despite the pitfalls, some Waldorf high schools introduce tenth graders to an ambitious course entitled the Bible as a Source of Literature. From the outset, our approach has been to avoid entirely this bitterly contested arena, where religious fervor and secular skepticism grapple for supremacy. Instead, we ask students to set aside their preconceptions, their catechisms, their devotion to or disdain of the Bible. This exercise, in and of itself, is a kind of lesson; it requires great effort to jettison personal views and aspire towards a higher, more objective ground.

One of the less controversial exercises we give tenth graders is to be on the lookout for famous biblical phrases that have inspired literary titles or that have become well-known axioms. Students usually compile a healthy list of book and play titles: Hemingway's *The Sun Also Rises* (Ecclesiastes 1:5), Steinbeck's *The Grapes of Wrath* (Deuteronomy 32:32) and *East of Eden* (Genesis 4:16), Uris' *Exodus*, Lawrence and Lee's *Inherit the Wind* (Proverbs 11:29), Wilder's *The Skin of Our Teeth* (Job 19:20), Hellman's *The Little Foxes* (Song of Songs 2:15), Heinlein's *Stranger in a Strange Land* (Exodus 2:22). The catalogue of familiar sayings originating in the Bible is formidable: "By the sweat of your brow" (Genesis 3:19); "Spare the rod and spoil the child" (Proverbs 13:24); "An eye for an eye" (Exodus 21:24); "My brother's keeper" (Genesis 4:9); "The apple of his eye" (Deuteronomy 32:10); "A man after his own heart" (Samuel 13:14); "Man doth not live by bread alone" (Deuteronomy 8:3 and Matthew 4:4); "The meek shall inherit the earth" (Matthew 5:5); "The spirit is willing, but the flesh is weak" (Matthew 26:41); "The blind leading the blind" (Matthew 15:14); "The truth shall set you free" (John 8:32); are only a few.

However, the more challenging task has been to delve into the rich and fertile recurring motifs informing the entire Bible. Taking our cue from the scholar Northrop Frye and his brilliant book *The Great Code: The Bible and Literature*, we examine the Bible as a literary unity. His premise is that the Old and New Testaments can be seen, literarily at least, as a cohesive whole; each one contains keys to understanding the other. Furthermore, he sees in both Testaments archetypal patterns and images that further interconnect the two. Students discover a fundamental pattern within the first two books of the Old Testament that actually presages the structure of the entire

Bible. Reading the stories of Adam and Eve, Noah, Abraham and Isaac, Joseph, and Moses, they recognize three general stages: an initial phase of stability and/or prosperity, followed by a decline into danger and/or hardships that lead to suffering, and finally some kind of deliverance that provides new hope and the possibility of restoration. If one were to diagram the movement, it would look like a "U"—what one student termed "a cosmic bathtub"—starting from a protected elevation, then tracing a descent into tribulations, followed by an ascent earned by surmounting various ordeals, until once again a summit is reached and good fortune re-established.

Adam and Eve begin in Eden, disobey God, are cast out of the Garden; they never regain paradise, but they find some measure of redemption by dint of their hard work, companionship, and ennobling mortality. Joseph is his father's favorite until his envious brothers conspire to sell him into slavery and make his disappearance look like a bloody death. After enduring an arduous journey to Egypt and incarceration because of a false accusation, Joseph displays his ability to interpret dreams that attracts the beneficence of the pharaoh. Joseph becomes vizier, a position that enables him to eventually reunite with, and forgive, his long-lost brethren. Moses is raised as an Egyptian prince until he kills an Egyptian taskmaster and discovers the secret of his Hebrew lineage. He goes into exile, is chosen by God to liberate his people, then suffers first his own doubts, then the collective doubts of the Israelites as they wander for forty years in the desert before arriving in the Promised Land.

Later in the Old Testament, the story of Job illustrates this pattern perfectly. He begins as a righteous, prosperous man, whose possessions, loving family and even his health are snatched away from him when he becomes a pawn in a betting contest between God and the devil. Yet, although he suffers, although he longs for death, Job refuses to "curse God and die." (Job 2:9) He tells his "comforters," "As God liveth, who hath taken away my judgment; and the Almighty, who hath vexed my soul; all the while my breath is in me, and the spirit of God is in my nostrils; my lips shall not speak wickedness nor my tongue utter deceit." (Job 27:2–4) In the end, Job's fidelity is rewarded—his health returned, his flocks doubled, a new family begotten, with seven sons and three daughters, and a long and newly blessed life still ahead.

This motif of good fortune, misfortune and renewal continues, of course, in the New Testament, most notably in the life of Jesus. Perhaps we can cite no greater or more grievous "turn of the wheel" than Jesus' plight as he goes from heralded healer, prophet and "king of the Jews" to crucified criminal. Yet the resurrection expands beyond the very limits of life this notion of restoration. Considering the cosmic sweep of the Old and New Testaments together, one can see the pattern encompass both the "alpha and the omega" of the Bible, for it begins and ends with visions of paradise. Interestingly, however, the New Jerusalem described at the end of Revelation is no uncultivated garden, but a walled city bejeweled and golden, where the tree of life reappears, whose leaves are for "the healing of the nations." (Revelation 22:2) Instead of Eden's serpent, the presence of The Lamb illuminates the city. After all the wayward paths and failings, all the ordeals and afflictions, God creates a heavenly domain where he "shall wipe away all tears from their eyes; and there shall be no more death, neither sorrow, nor crying, neither shall there be any more pain; for the formers things are passed away." (Revelation 21:4)

Eden and New Jerusalem are not the only images that seem to echo one another in the Old and New Testaments. If students can accept Frye's contention that the essential crux of the Old Testament is about the fate of a *people* (the Hebrew descendents of Abraham and Sarah), and the New Testament is the story of an *individual*, they can also begin to discover some interesting parallels between the plight of the Israelites and the life of Jesus. One example focuses on two prominent Josephs. In Genesis, after forgiving his brothers, Joseph guides his father Jacob and his entire family to Egypt to escape the ravages of famine in Canaan. In the New Testament, Joseph, husband of Mary, leads his wife and child to Egypt to escape the "slaughter of the innocents." Jacob's sons engender the twelve tribes of Israel; Jesus' twelve disciples spread the gospel that becomes Christianity. Water plays a crucial role in saving the Israelites from the pursuing Egyptians (the parting of the Red Sea); in the New Testament, water acquires the capacity to "save" souls through the power of baptism.

Then there are fascinating Moses/Jesus correspondences. Moses receives "The Law" on a mountain, while Jesus delivers a new version of "The Law" on a mountain (The Sermon on the Mount). Moses is on Mount Sinai forty days and nights before receiving the Ten Commandments; Jesus goes to the wilderness for forty days and nights where he encounters, and rejects, the blandishments of Satan. When he descends the mountain "with the two tables of testimony in his hand...Moses wist not that the skin of his face shone while he talked with them." (Exodus 34:29)—in other words, he is transfigured; in the New Testament, "Jesus taketh Peter, James and John his brother, and bringeth them up into a high mountain apart, and was transfigured before them: and his face did shine as the sun, and his raiment was white as the light." (Matthew 17:1–2) Interestingly, at this juncture, none other than Moses (with Elias) appears with Jesus. Moses performs miracles in the desert when he "smites" the rock with his rod and water issues forth for the parched, disquieted Israelites; Jesus performs a similar miracle when he multiplies the "loaves and fishes" to feed the multitudes. One clever student even found another dubious but "punny" parallel: "Jesus heals plagues, while Moses plagues heels!" (presumably the Egyptians).

Although this last correspondence is a bit of a stretch, throughout the entire course, we encourage sophomores to look for patterns throughout the Bible. Through this type of active, relational thinking, the students revel in finding correlations and congruencies, in tracing the development of an image as archetypal as a lamb or goat, water or fire through Old and New Testaments. The same holds true for primal themes: the fate of the firstborn, overweening human ambition, divine judgment, revenge, the nature of the law.

This last topic can be the springboard for sophomores to discuss yet again the all-important idea of an evolving human consciousness. They recognize that in the Old Testament, the Lord is a stern, exacting taskmaster, who issues commandments and dispenses punishments as a strict father might treat his children. Indeed, the "children" of Israel repeatedly demonstrate a waywardness and rebelliousness characteristic of the immature. They seem incapable of leading themselves; they need the firm hand of an authoritarian God, or of an equally demanding leader of Moses' ilk. Furthermore they seem to respect the Law only when it comes with the most severe consequences. The very phrasing of so many of the Ten Commandments—"Thou shalt not"—suggests a divine lawgiver who believes his "children" require the strongest strictures and who will brook no disobedience.

By contrast, the students see the New Testament's Son of Man as a gentler, more accessible presence, preaching a new Law. "Love your enemies, bless them that curse you" (Matthew 5:44) and "Whosoever shall smite thee on thy right cheek, turn to him to the other also" (Matthew 5:39) are a far cry from the "eye for an eye" revenge required in Exodus. The law of the Old Testament is like a hammer wielded from above; the law of the New Testament arrives as a seed from a "sower" who walks among his people. More insightful tenth graders will discover that this new law does not descend from on high, but rather issues from within. One particularly bright girl wrote about the movement from outer to inner as reflected in the depiction of sacrifice in Old and New Testaments. She noted that as early as the Abraham and Isaac episode, we can see how the ram becomes the external, substitute sacrifice for the son. However, in the New Testament, the primary reference to sheep is "The Son" himself, now also "The Lamb," who is "sacrificed" on behalf of all of humanity.

As with all the other courses in the Waldorf curriculum, we teachers need to resist the temptation to become overly zealous sermonizers. The "phenomenological" approach that allows the teeming biblical images and themes to speak of their own accord yields a far richer harvest than some teacher's pronouncements. Tenth graders do not generally need, or appreciate, having parallels drawn between their adolescent phase of life and some biblical equivalent. They sense intuitively the gradual movement in their own lives from outer compulsion towards inner freedom, even if they do not quite yet understand how to surmount the inner conflicts they will inevitably encounter as eleventh and twelfth graders in order to become ever-more themselves.

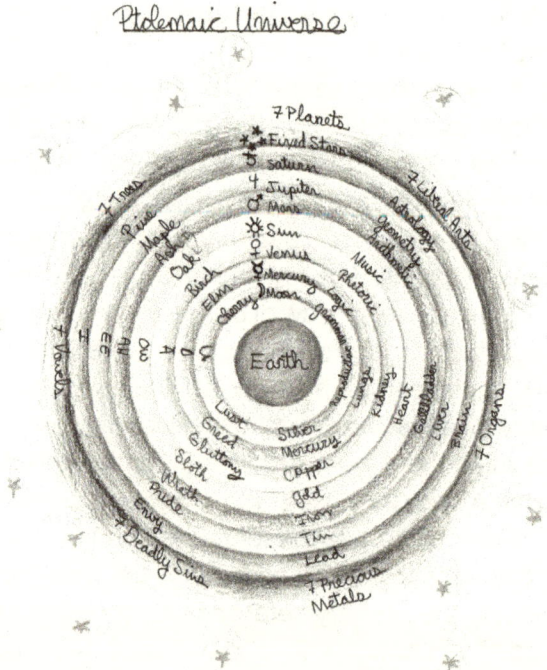

Figure 5 – Classwork during Dante *main lesson*

Eleventh Grade:
The Journey Towards Selfhood

The Dark Night of the Soul

What happens to eleventh graders? Why do so many of these ex-sophomores, who were so full of themselves, who, just a few months previously, had exhibited a kind of bluster and swagger and smugness, now in eleventh grade find themselves stricken by some malaise that could be termed a "Dark Night of the Soul"?

Some time ago a mother of one of my eleventh grade students met with me and shared her concerns that her formerly happy-go-lucky, genial, mountain-biking son had become evasive, burdened, non-communicative, reclusive—almost a stranger to his own mother. Now this was a single mother describing her only son; she was naturally worried that these changes in him might indicate some deep psychological problem. Was some heretofore hidden hurt about some past childhood trauma bubbling to the surface? Was he using drugs? Had something happened at school between him and his classmates?

So I took Mark aside and spent lunch one day talking to him about his experience of being a junior. Mark is a wonderful fellow who always appears to have just woken up; in fact, he always looks as if he's just slept in his clothes. But underneath that rumpled exterior is a very astute and articulate young man. Yet when I asked him to describe what he'd been feeling this past fall, he was initially at a loss for words. Is it so surprising that young people can't always express what they're experiencing at the moment? It reminds me of the saying, "We don't know who discovered water, but we're pretty sure it wasn't a fish." How can we expect them to have much perspective about the very air they breathe, the state of soul that envelops them?

Nevertheless, Mark was able to describe his recent despondency as "a kind of funk. I've been in a haze." Then he said something as true of the eleventh grade experience as any I've heard. He said simply, "I've gone inside." He went on to say that he didn't know if it was a good or bad thing, but that he found himself wandering inwardly. Mark had begun to discover that he had more inner chambers than he had ever realized before, and he was becoming more and more interested in what made himself tick.

Douglas Gerwin, widely known Waldorf lecturer and a long-time colleague, once characterized this inner exploration in the following manner. Picture a young person, sixteen or seventeen years old wandering through a large house. She strolls through familiar rooms, looks out to vistas she has known since childhood. Then she notices and opens a door to a wing of the house she never knew existed. She walks down a dark and unfamiliar corridor, her breathing quickening; without warning, she feels the floorboards beneath her give way. She lands painfully in an even darker, dungeon-like basement, surrounded by eerie shadows and strange, chilling noises. This is akin to the inner "soul-scape" experienced by so many juniors—a sudden descent into dark, even forbidding chambers that nevertheless beckon to young people, no matter how awful the potential revelations might be.

During this "Dark Night of the Soul," it seems clear that eleventh graders suffer. Among other afflictions, this can manifest as a deeply felt crisis in confidence. I had a tearful meeting with a girl in my junior class earlier in the fall (*she* was the one crying), about how hard everything in her life had become. She was certain that she was the only one in the class who took six hours to do her homework, that for all her efforts she was the only one rewarded with mediocre marks. I had nearly the exact same conversation with two of her classmates within a week. Besides putting them in touch with one another, which may have provided some measure of consolation to discover fellow sufferers, I really tried to resist the impulse to somehow make these students' struggles less painful. Sadistic as this sounds, all this angst in the eleventh grade may be both inevitable and, in a certain way, even desirable.

It is no accident that in Waldorf schools around the world, juniors experience Dante the Pilgrim as he descends apprehensively into the pit of the living dead; they also encounter Parzival, as he stands publicly shamed by Cundrie in the midst of the Arthurian circle, and Hamlet as he torments himself with doubts about a rightful course of action. These three figures form the core of an eleventh grade literature curriculum whose themes embody what I would call "the transformational" on the one hand, and "the relational" on the other.

Figure 4 – Classwork during Dante *main lesson*

To return to Baravalle's words—if indeed the curriculum should arise out of an insightful assessment of young people's real needs, then we should be able to see in the students themselves some recognizable need for the transformational and the relational. The conversations I just mentioned provide one glimpse; as indicated in the last chapter, students' writing provides another. This poem was written by a junior over twenty years ago, but that only testifies to its transcendent quality.

The Plum

Like the pit of a dying plum
I am wrapped in pulp—
Pulp thought, pulp dream, (prison pulp)
Sour-sweet, red and soft.
I offer my dream to you;
I pass the plum around,
Hoping from the middle,
From that small, wood-encrusted bone,
To be scraped clean of meat...
To be eaten.
Inside the pit there is a seed—
Just a hint of greatness.
But still you hold the fruit of me
And squeeze the dream
And praise me for my juiciness
And never touch the pit
And never find the seed
And only lick the purple skin.[37]
– Laura Fisher '85

This poem is potent at least in part because it really expresses three central truths about the eleventh grade experience: (1) sixteen/seventeen-year-olds can feel inwardly trapped ("prison pulp") by circumstances not entirely of their own making. (2) They sense within themselves simultaneously a dying and a renewing (the "dying plum" as well as "a seed/just a hint of greatness"). The poem is an expression of the newly liberated astral forces bringing with them a fledgling but still acute consciousness of childhood dying away and of new possibilities opening up. (3) Juniors can feel completely unrecognized, misapprehended by, but very concerned about, the other, the "you" in the poem, who holds and squeezes and praises the outer appearances, but never really delves to find the essential person within. The poet is nearly bursting with a longing to be recognized by the other—that is the relational aspect. She also hopes to be "scraped clean of meat, to be eaten," the ultimate transformation.

So we need to find stories that contain at their core themes touching on the transformational and the relational. What we are really talking about here are initiation stories. Earlier I referred to the curriculum as providing mini-initiations for young people who meet some reflection of their own inner experiences in the literature they explore and the scientific phenomena they observe. Linda Sussman, in her wonderful recent book entitled *The Speech of the Grail*, describes the path of initiation as a threefold process. In the first stage, the questing individual must go through a separation, a departure from everything familiar and comforting—from family and friends, from traditions and well-worn beliefs. In other words, he or she must enter a realm of uncertainty. She quotes from Eliot's "Four Quartets" a passage that could almost serve as an anthem in praise of uncertainty.

East Coker (excerpt)

Shall I say it again? In order to arrive there,
To arrive where you are, to get from where you are not,
You must go by a way wherein there is no ecstasy.

> In order to arrive at what you do not know
> You must go by a way which is the way of ignorance.
> In order to possess what you do not possess
> You must go by the way of dispossession.
> In order to arrive at what you are not
> You must go through the way in which you are not.
> And what you do not know is the only thing you know.
> And what you own is what you do not own.
> And where you are is where you are not.[38]

If an individual can somehow make his or her peace with this soul condition, this often terrifying state of irresolution, the traveler next undergoes a series of ordeals, designed to test the mettle and resolve, resiliency and resourcefulness of the neophyte. This is the second stage, and here the timeless story of Gilgamesh provides an epic panorama of such initiation.

Gilgamesh: The Story of Becoming Human

The ancient tale of Gilgamesh was recorded on seventh century B.C. clay tablets that were uncovered in Ninevah, one time the capital of the Assyrian empire, by nineteenth century archaeologists. However, evidence points to much earlier versions dating back to the third millennium B.C., making *Gilgamesh* one of humanity's oldest and most enduring recorded stories. In the Waldorf high school, students often read the epic in tenth grade during their exploration of ancient cultures. However, the questing nature of the story can also serve as a bridge into those eleventh grade themes touching on the transformational and relational. We usually have students read the tale in the summer before their junior year, because at its heart, Gilgamesh examines what it means to be a human being and the journey it requires to "become human."

The story revolves around two figures: Gilgamesh, king of Uruk, who is part god, part man, and Enkidu, who is part animal, part man. At the outset of the narrative, Gilgamesh is an arrogant tyrant suffering from the ennui of having no real purpose in life. He amuses himself by sleeping with brides on their wedding nights, but such intimacies only leave him feeling isolated and empty.

> I have never known such weariness, before,
> As if some life in me has disappeared
> Or needs to be filled up again.
> I am alone and I have longed
> For some companionship. My people
> Also have grown tired of my solitude.[39]

Far from Gilgamesh's decadent court, Enkidu runs with the animals,

> Not knowing fear or wisdom.
> He freed them from the traps
> The hunters set.[40]

When word reaches Gilgamesh about this wild man, he agrees to have a woman seduce Enkidu to "make the animals ashamed of him."[41] The seduction works and, reminiscent of Adam and Eve's awakening to their nakedness after eating the forbidden apple, Enkidu finds himself now cut off from his previous life.

> When he rose again
> Looking for his friends who had gone,
> He felt a strange exhaustion,
> As if life had left his body.
> He felt their absence. ...His friend
> Had left him to a vast aloneness
> He had never felt before.[42]

Enkidu hears about the king's custom of sleeping with the virgin brides and some moral outrage swells in him, leading him into Uruk to thwart Gilgamesh's plans. When he finds his way to the newest bride's chamber blocked, Gilgamesh lunges at Enkidu and a titanic wrestling match ensues. Neither man can subdue the other; at the point of exhaustion, Gilgamesh leans against his opponent

> and looked into his eyes
> And saw himself in the other,
> Just as Enkidu saw himself in Gilgamesh.
> In the silence of the people they began to laugh
> And clutched each other in their breathless exultation.[43]

This moment becomes a wonderful lesson for students to consider. How does hand-to-hand, mortal combat lead to the start of a lifelong friendship? A number of juniors shared their own experiences of this reversal; one girl described a long-standing enmity she had had for a classmate that came to a boil over a relatively small incident. A harsh and hurtful shouting match followed, resulting in both parties breaking down in tears. Their mutual weeping led to a recognition of the other person's vulnerability and a real conversation about their differences, which resulted in a growing understanding of the other's situation and, shortly thereafter, a budding friendship. Students agreed that this dynamic of angry argument eventually transforming into an empathetic connection seemed quite common. However, many juniors also agreed that precipitating such confrontations (in other words, speaking their minds) required a level of courage and trust in the process that teenagers do not often possess.

The unlikely friendship between Gilgamesh and Enkidu deepens as they undertake perilous adventures together. Still suffering from overweening pride, Gilgamesh convinces Enkidu to accompany him to the forest of Humbaba and to kill that monstrous guardian of the sacred trees,

> to prove
> Him not the awesome thing we think he is
> And that the boundaries set up by gods
> Are not unbreakable.[44]

This universal motif of human beings overreaching the limits set by divine forces can be found in cultural parables around the world, in the West, most notably in the biblical stories of Adam and Eve, the tower of Babel, and the Greeks' cautionary account of Daedalus and Icarus. Like the figures in these tales, Gilgamesh and Enkidu pay a heavy price for their hubris. Enkidu is fatally wounded in the fight with Humbaba. Gilgamesh, now vulnerable in his newly caring state, is inconsolable after Enkidu dies. He resolves to go in search of the secret to eternal life and thereby bring his friend back from the dead.

Now Gilgamesh enters a realm familiar to readers of initiation stories; he persuades the Scorpion people who guard the gates into the afterlife to let him pass. Like the myriad mythological and religious figures who journey to the land of the dead—Odysseus, Aeneas, Dionysus, Hercules, Ishtar, Krishna, Orpheus, Persephone, even Jesus—Gilgamesh crosses this momentous threshold. He enters the ironically named Road of the Sun, "Which was so shrouded in darkness/That he could see neither/What was ahead of him nor behind."[45] With his grief as his only companion, Gilgamesh finds himself standing before a valley gleaming with precious stones and "fruit-filled vines."[46] Suddenly he is overcome with the pain of loss; before such beauty, Enkidu's absence cuts deeper than any anguish Gilgamesh has felt before.

During his journey Gilgamesh vacillates between despair and rage at the seeming injustice of his plight. "He felt himself now singled out for loss/Apart from everyone else."[47] He rejects comfort and aid from a barmaid and a boatman; in his fury, "Coming upon some stones that stood in his way/He smashed them into a thousand pieces."[48] Eleventh graders have no trouble relating to Gilgamesh's angst. They understand his soul distress and his anger. Many must cope with both on a daily basis. In fact, most people confronted with the inevitability of death experience emotional extremes.

Despite his outbursts, he finally crosses the Sea of Death to receive the counsel of the wise Utnapishtim, a Noah-like divinity who has survived a catastrophic flood. When Gilgamesh beseeches Utnapishtim to give him the secret to eternal life, Utnapishtim delivers an exquisite description of the human condition.

> Friendship is vowing toward immortality
> And does not know the passing away of beauty
> (Though take care!)
> Because it aims for the spirit.
> Many years ago through loss I learned
> That love is wrung from our inmost heart
> Until only the loved one is and we are not...
> I think love's kiss kills our heart of flesh.
> It is the only way to eternal life,
> Which should be unbearable if lived
> Among the dying flowers
> And the shrieking farewells
> Of the overstretched arms of our spoiled hopes.[49]

Students grapple with the meaning of this passage, since they recognize its relevance to the question of what it means to be human. How can they make sense of the paradoxical statement that "love's kiss kills our heart of flesh./It is the only way to eternal life"? They begin to see, even before Gilgamesh does, that eternal life is attainable only in the domain of the spiritual, not the earthly. Utnapishtim's words about the nature of true friendship also impress many young people who live in a world of constantly shifting alliances, ephemeral relationships and often trifling concerns. Waldorf teachers welcome any experience that deepens the perspective of our generally privileged and pampered students.

Sometimes life itself can reinforce such lessons. Back in the early '90s, during the crisis in the Balkans, Green Meadow partnered with a local Sufi mosque to rescue a number of young people from the war zone. The mosque found families for the Bosnian youths, and the school offered full scholarships. The impact these teenagers had on the entire school community was palpable from the beginning. Gifted, earnest and articulate, these Bosnian students also brought with them a boundless appreciation for their new opportunities, as well as a deep-seated concern for the families and friends they had left behind. At an All-Souls' Day assembly in the late fall, one eleventh grade girl named Fatima asked to read a letter she had composed to her best friend back in Bosnia, after she had died in a bombing of a marketplace several months earlier. Her words left many in the audience weeping as she expressed her abiding affection for her friend and her heartfelt wish for the violence in her country to end. In an American culture that seems to promote superficiality in its young people, Fatima's open letter had an immediate and sobering effect. Suddenly one student's concern about looking fat in her homecoming dress and another's anxiety about his recent parking ticket seemed quite trivial beside Fatima's profound sorrow. During the years that these Bosnian students attended Green Meadow, they helped to broaden and deepen the lives of their teachers and classmates.

The Bosnians have long since graduated, but *Gilgamesh* has remained a staple of the eleventh grade curriculum to stimulate questions about life, death and the nature of friendship. Returning to the story: Gilgamesh is dissatisfied with Utnapishtim's answer and continues to plead for some tangible "antidote" that will bring Enkidu back from the dead. Utnapishtim finally relents.

> I will tell you a secret I have never told,
> Something to take back with you and guard.
> There is a plant in the river. Its thorns
> Will prick your hands as a rose thorn pricks
> But it will give to you new life.[50]

A close reading of the passage reveals that Utnapishtim's secret does not ensure *Enkidu's* return to the living, but rather promises to give *Gilgamesh* "new life." And, indeed, this transformation comes to pass, but only after a surprising twist. Gilgamesh loses the miracle plant when he leaves it unguarded; a serpent devours it and leaves behind its own discarded skin. After weeping at yet another loss, Gilgamesh sheds his own skin, in a manner of speaking. He returns to Uruk, no longer the bored, arrogant tyrant untouched by human feelings, but neither is he the self-pitying mourner.

> Gilgamesh said nothing more
> To force his sorrow on another.
> He looked at the walls,
> Awed at the heights
> His people had achieved
> And for a moment—just a moment—
> All that lay behind him
> Passed from view.[51]

The awe that he feels offers a glimmer of hope that Gilgamesh has suffered enough to rule his subjects in the future guided by compassion and decency.

The end of the story is a perfect time to introduce students to the life of Elisabeth Kubler-Ross, and to the five stages of grief that she has chronicled in her work with the terminally ill. Juniors see immediately that Kubler-Ross' stages suggest some archetypal experience, because even the central character in a five-thousand-year-old epic undergoes each one in the aftermath of Enkidu's death. They can identify when he goes through the initial stage of *denial*, refusing to believe in the finality of death. On a number of occasions he is possessed by an uncontrollable *anger*, erupting at the Scorpion people, Siduri the Barmaid, Urshanabi the boatman. Kubler-Ross describes a third stage that she calls *bargaining*; in this phase, individuals facing death will want to strike a deal with the Almighty. So they plead with God to shrink the tumor, make the illness disappear, restore them to health. In return, they vow to lead a better life—to go to church or temple weekly, to pray regularly, to treat people more kindly. Gilgamesh's bargaining is implicit; he implores the gods to help him "win eternal life,"[52] and with newfound wisdom, he will work to redeem his "spoiled youth."[53] Gilgamesh succumbs to the fourth stage—*depression*, even despair, as described above—intermittently on his journey, but finally he comes to an *acceptance* of death after the loss of the rose-like plant and his decision to return home.

This acceptance can be meaningful only after a person has endured life-changing ordeals, according to Sussman's description of initiation. Gilgamesh suffers deeply by coming to grips with the essential differences between mortal and immortal realms. "A man sees death in things./That is what it is like to be a man."[54] At the same time he begins to understand why Utnapishtim, this divine figure on the far side of the Sea of Death, confides to Gilgamesh,

> I would grieve
> At all that may befall you still
> If I did not know you must return
> And bury your own loss and build
> Your world anew with your own hands.
> I envy you your freedom.[55]

The gods may enjoy immortality, but only human beings seem to have the freedom to shape and reshape their own lives.

It is worth reminding eleventh graders that undergoing trials such as Gilgamesh encounters is never a passive experience; rather, it requires courage, openness, and tremendous inner activity to attain a measure of equilibrium. Another initiation story—Dante's account of one individual's descent into hell—offers students yet another glimpse of a man's encounters in the afterlife and the qualities he must develop if he is to unite with his higher self.

Dante's *Divine Comedy*: Sins of Fire, Sins of Ice

As perhaps the highest literary expression ever describing a path of salvation (except possibly the Bible), *The Inferno* provides a wonderful picture of the sobering consequences of astrality gone amok. From the punishments for the sins of incontinence in upper hell to the agonies experienced by the traitors in the ninth circle, Dante's Pilgrim has to confront one nightmarish vision after another. He has to learn to stifle his natural sympathies for the sinners, to overcome his fear, and to listen to the rational voice of his guide Virgil if he is to have a hope of ever finding the right path again.

Figure 6 – Classwork during Dante *main lesson*

Of course, it is not initially so easy for twenty-first century students to relate to Dante's grand imagination of the afterlife. In an age where moral relativism holds sway, Dante's vision seems rigidly orthodox, not unlike today's resurgence of religious fundamentalism that encourages a return to absolutes. At the very least, we want students to understand the medieval mind that could create such a vision. Dante (1265–1321) lived in a world ordered by The Great Chain of Being, a cosmic hierarchy stretching from the throne of God down through the ranks of angelic beings and the feudal classes of humanity, through the realms of the animals and plants to the mineral kingdom. In such a vertical chain, one's station and "linkage" were its defining features, each link connected to a superior and inferior segment. From highest to lowest, distinctions were made between the more and less valued; yet everything had its place in the Great Chain. "Intelligent design" was not some debatable point; it was experienced at every level. What such a system lacked in terms of freedom and mobility, it compensated for by providing security and a sense of belonging.

Furthermore, the entire universe was interwoven by correspondences. Each of the traditional seven planetary bodies was an expression of divine forces and, in turn, exerted unique influences upon the earth. For example, the moon was connected to silver in the realm of the metals, to the color lavender, to the cherry tree, to the reproductive organs in the human being and to lust among the seven deadly sins; Mars was related to iron, the color red, the oak, the gall bladder, and to wrath; Venus, to copper, the color green, the birch, the kidney, and to gluttony.

Even after becoming acquainted with this medieval web ordering all of creation, students often still cannot completely fathom the architecturally perfect design that Dante gives to the afterlife. After an introductory canto, Dante devotes thirty-three cantos each to his depictions of hell, purgatory and paradise. Each of the three divisions is further separated into discrete subdivisions, and each ends with the word "stars." Furthermore, every line Dante writes is eleven syllables in length, the middle line of every three-line stanza rhyming with the first and third lines of the following stanza in an interweaving *terza rima*. Unquestionably Dante wants his readers to feel that the soul's journey after death proceeds according to the same divine plan and inexorable laws that govern life on earth.

From the first canto of *The Inferno*, Dante makes clear that it is not the world order that is out of balance, but the Pilgrim, who has lost his way.

> *Nel mezzo del cammin di nostra vita*
> *Mi retrovai per una selva oscura*
> *Che la diritta via era smarrita.*
>
> Midway along the journey of our life
> I woke to find myself in a dark wood
> For I had wandered off from the straight path.[56]

Students see right away that Dante intends his scope to be more universal than particular, as evidenced by his deliberate reference to "our life," instead of "my life." He is explicitly inviting readers to identify with the Pilgrim's experience. Furthermore, when the Pilgrim's path is blocked almost immediately by three animals—a ravenous wolf, a furious lion, and a gaudy leopard—students begin to see metaphorical possibilities. Like the figure of Virgil, who guides the Pilgrim along this journey through the expanses of the afterlife, Dante guides eleventh graders into a world replete not only with levels of sinners but with levels of meaning. Soon enough they will recognize that each of the beasts represents a region of the Inferno: the wolf, upper hell, where the sins of appetite are punished; the lion, the mid-levels where the perpetrators of violence suffer; and the leopard, the lowest reaches where the architects of fraud live in eternal agony.

As the Pilgrim and Virgil descend—through limbo where the unbaptized reside, through the upper regions where the souls of the lustful, gluttonous, avaricious, slothful and wrathful all appear—students begin to appreciate the thought Dante has put into punishing his sinners. In every circle, Dante has created a horrific environment specifically devised to intensify the wrongdoers' torments. The lustful must contend with whipping, tempestuous winds; the slothful are submerged in the black muck of a swamp. Furthermore, Dante metes out punishments that seem diabolically designed both to mirror the sins and to maximize their consequences. The uncommitted in the vestibule, who "lived a life/but lived it with no blame and with no praise,"[57] are forced to rush around waving banners while swarms of hornets and wasps continually sting them into perpetual movement. The spendthrifts and hoarders in the fourth circle must strain eternally to roll enormous boulders into one another, while the wrathful are condemned to wage hand-to-hand combat, tearing each other "limb from limb."[58]

Each circle of hell also has its own appropriate guardians who oversee, and occasionally even mete out, the punishments. Cerberus, the ravenous three-headed dog from Greek mythology, presides over the gluttons.

> His eyes are red, his beard is slobbered black,
> His belly swollen, and he has claws for hands,
> He rips the spirits, flays and mangles them.[59]

The Minotaur, "gone crazy with the fever of his rage,"[60] and centaurs, armed with bows and arrows, rule the region of the seventh circle, where the violent, "sunken to their eyelids," [61] writhe in a boiling river of blood. Far below, where the fraudulent inhabit the eighth circle, horned devils lash the backs of the seducers and hypocrites, the liars and thieves.

Most students are fascinated by these ingenious punishments, especially as the criteria behind Dante's ordering of the Inferno become increasingly apparent. The transgressors in upper hell are victims of their own uncontrollable urges. They cannot master their will impulses, but because their sins lack premeditation, Dante accords them a less ignominious position in the underworld, relatively speaking, than the more malicious souls below. The perpetrators of violence inhabiting mid-hell have also allowed their passions to overcome them, but their impulsive deeds have turned bloody. Since, in Dante's eyes, only God can rightfully take a human life, those who play God end up in the seventh circle of hell.

When we descend into the lower realms of the Inferno, we meet sinners who at first glance would not merit such harsh punishment. Why would thieves and hypocrites be considered more despicable sinners than murderers? For Dante, the key is intentionality. Any human being who has *deliberately* exploited others has earned a place among the other vile, fraudulent denizens of the eighth circle. They have taken God's most precious gift to human beings—rationality—and perverted it for their own selfish ends. The greater the deceit—the more far-reaching the damage to others—the deeper into hell plunges the sinner. Therefore, it is not so shocking to find the traitorous in the lowest reaches of hell. What *is* initially surprising is *how* they suffer in this pit, for here we see not a raging inferno of flames everlastingly consuming screaming souls, but a vast, arctic landscape.

Scattered like "straws worked into glass,/Some lying flat, some perpendicular/either with their heads up or their feet/and some bent head to foot shaped like a bow,"[62] countless traitors lie encased in ice. One tormented soul gnaws at the skull of another. In the center of the lake stands the ultimate betrayer—the giant, imprisoned figure of Lucifer. Far from the imposing divinity whose fall from heaven actually created the cavernous inferno, Dante's Lucifer is a pathetic sight. He has three faces, and in each mouth Dante has stuffed one of three traitors to be eternally devoured: Brutus, Cassius, and Judas, each of whom betrayed his benefactor. The lake is virtually silent, except for the muffled cries of anguish from above, and the ceaseless creaking of Lucifer's enormous, windmill wings, which perpetuate the arctic conditions by continually fanning the glacial air.

After reading this horrifying scene, one student recalled Robert Frost's poem "Fire and Ice."

> Some say the world will end in fire,
> Some say in ice.
> From what I've tasted of desire
> I hold with those who favor fire.
> But if it had to perish twice,
> I think I know enough of hate
> To say that for destruction ice
> Is also great
> And would suffice.[63]

Fire has its function in Dante's hell: in burning tombs torturing the heretics of the sixth circle; in the flakes of fire that rain down perpetually on the blasphemers, sodomites, and usurers in the desert of the seventh circle; and in the flames that lick the soles of those sinners stuck upside down in baptismal fonts, simonists who fraudulently sold ecclesiastical offices. Yet it is an icebound landscape that Dante reserves for the most heinous sinners of all. What more appropriate environment could he have chosen to illustrate the catastrophic consequences of cold, intellectual scheming unmoved by the warmth of human sympathies?

What is the intended effect of this journey into hell with our eleventh graders? Are we privately hoping that because of their experience reading about Francesca's and Paolo's eternal embrace in the tempestuous second circle, our hot and hormonal students will swear off lust, or that our broody melancholics will abjure all thoughts of suicide once they read about those tormented souls trapped in trees in the seventh circle? Or that the thieves among us will think twice about coveting others' property when they see how Dante condemns his light-fingered contemporaries to endlessly exchange their human forms for those of snakes?

Today's teenagers seem far less susceptible than Dante's citizenry to the threat of eternal damnation. It is more likely that eleventh graders will at least consider in a fresh way what a sin is, and whether Dante's rankings regarding the gravity of each sin agree with their own. One extraordinarily bright student several years ago reacted angrily to what she saw as Dante's narrow-minded, condemnatory thinking. The whole idea of "sinning" seemed outmoded to her. Yet she triggered a fruitful discussion about the difference between a sin and a crime, and whether God needed to "pile on" eternal consequences after we mortals have already suffered the consequences exacted by courts or consciences here on earth.

One assignment that enables students to bridge the gulf between Dante's medieval thinking and their own is to have them identify some modern variation of the seven deadly sins. Then we ask them to compose a canto describing their sinners in hell. Using *The Inferno* as a template, they write in some approximation of *terza rima*, complete with a fitting environment and guardian, and some diabolically clever punishment. They write cantos about DVD and CD pirates, contemporary counterfeiters, child abusers, sex slave traders, sweatshop exploiters, corporate polluters, advertising executives who try to sell young girls on the idea that they have to be "runway model emaciated" or Britney buxom to be attractive.

Like Dante's pilgrim, eleventh graders have usually had enough of hell by the time they encounter Lucifer in the frozen pit. Yet even though we introduce them to the hopeful souls who labor on the terraces of Mount Purgatory, even though we finally offer students a brief glimpse of the Pilgrim's encounter with his beatific Beatrice and his stunning heavenly vision, it is the darker, almost visceral torments of *The Inferno* that haunt students long after they have put down the book.

As with many initiation experiences, the most demanding ordeals often leave the most lasting impressions. Sussman suggests that if the trials are successfully surmounted, one usually finds initiates returning "home," now ennobled and, on some fundamental level, transformed by the tribulations endured. However, the initiation is rarely for the benefit of the individual alone; rather, the returning initiate shares the bounty of his/her achievements with those he/she left behind, so that the entire community is enriched and enlarged. This motif is as ancient as fairy tales and epics such as the aforementioned *Gilgamesh* and *The Odyssey,* but also as modern as Paton's *Cry, the Beloved Country,* Leslie Marmon Silko's *Ceremony,* Charles Frazier's *Cold Mountain* and Tolkien's classic *Lord of the Rings* trilogy. And we find it most profoundly in Wolfram von Eschenbach's timeless story *Parzival.*

Parzival: The Quest within the Question

It is always helpful to teach the story of Parzival after Dante's *Divine Comedy,* even though the former was composed at the beginning of the thirteenth century, a hundred years before Dante's masterpiece. The latter is really the highest expression of a bygone age, a grand vision of a divinely ordered universe, encompassing the life of the spirit after death. By contrast, *Parzival* may be set in a medieval world of knights and castles, but it is a remarkably prescient and contemporary tale about the striving of human beings to bring spiritual values to life on earth in the modern age.

It begins as so many archetypal stories do, with the death of a king, Parzival's grandfather, and chronicles the adventures of Parzival's father Gahmuret as a valiant young knight. Deprived of an inheritance, he leaves his native land to find fame and fortune in the East. After successfully defending the kingdom of a beautiful, dark-skinned queen, Gahmuret falls in love with and marries Belacane. Then, after only a few weeks of domesticity, Gahmuret leaves his now-pregnant wife and returns to Europe as the appetite for jousting returns. This restlessness becomes Gahmuret's signature characteristic, the one obvious flaw in an otherwise exemplary knight. He enters a tournament, vanquishes all combatants, and wins the hand of yet another beautiful queen. However, the pattern of Gahmuret's life repeats itself: he marries Herzeloyde—his former marriage to a "heathen" considered null and void—then leaves her with child as he once again surrenders to his wanderlust. He travels back to the East, where he dies in battle, the victim of treachery when a villain covertly pours goat's blood on Gahmuret's diamond helmet, rendering it spongy and susceptible to any blow from a weapon.

Gahmuret's life and untimely death offer a host of portents to illuminate the subsequent adventures of Parzival. The most obvious link is Parzival's royal and knightly bloodline; his father is renowned in both East and West as the greatest champion of his generation. Another is the mysterious half-brother—son of the union of the black queen Belacane and Gahmuret—unknown to Parzival until their momentous encounter towards the end of the story. A third theme is the legacy of restlessness with which Parzival will also have to contend. Beyond all of these is the unfinished web of East/West strands traced by Gahmuret's travels back and forth between these regions. One perceptive student noted that Gahmuret's original coat of arms was the panther, but that he had replaced it with the symbol of the anchor, perhaps as an acknowledgment of his need for grounding and steadfastness. This student also made the inspired observation that the sign of the anchor is really a melding of Eastern and Western symbols—the cross, which was the emblem of Christian Europe, with the crescent moon so sacred to Arab cultures.

Figure 7 – *Classwork during* Parzival *main lesson*

On some level, Gahmuret must have experienced his mission as the uniting of East and West. However, he fails in this endeavor, and the striking image of the goat's blood softening the diamond helmet points to one possible reason. The crystal clarity of the diamond suggests a connection to the activity of thinking, an impression reinforced by the helmet's function as "head protector." Gahmuret was a great warrior, but his thinking was unsound, still in the service of his love of jousting. To act as unifier between two such diverse cultures, Gahmuret needed an enlightened thinking beyond his capacities. As is often the case, the father's mission would fall to the son to fulfill.

Gahmuret's death was the single biggest influence on Parzival through his childhood, despite the fact that Parzival never heard a word about his father during his formative years. Herzeloyde is heartbroken over the loss of her husband (her name literally means "heart's sorrow"); she determines that her son will never be exposed to the knowledge of knighthood and therefore never suffer his father's fate. So she retreats with Parzival (she doesn't even tell him his true name, instead calling him only "*bon fils, cher fils, beau fils*") into the seclusion of Soltane, a forest far removed from court intrigues and chivalric codes. Parzival spends his childhood in absolute ignorance of his lineage and of the larger world, until one day when three knights speed past him on their steeds. Nearly blinded by the light glinting off their armor and thinking them gods, Parzival resolves to become a knight and tells his mother of his newfound calling. Sensing the futility of preventing him from meeting his destiny, Herzeloyde acquiesces, but dresses her son in fool's apparel and gives him intentionally foolish advice. Her hope is the world will treat him so unkindly that he will return to her before more serious misfortune befalls him.

Students love to discuss Herzeloyde's misguided child-rearing strategy, comparing it to the overprotective practices certain parents employ to "quarantine" their teenagers today. One junior accused her parents of turning her into a movie addict by preventing her from seeing any films until she was twelve years old. Another expressed resentment about the way his mother would keep track of his social life by calling every friend's house he claimed to be visiting. Still other students defended Herzeloyde's intentions, if not the extremity of her plan, to shield her son from the world's perils. Most eleventh graders agree that young people should not be granted some carte blanche freedom to live their lives without any parental boundaries. It seems healthy to have these adolescents consider difficult child-rearing questions from the parents' point of view: What would be their family policy regarding television-watching? Would they allow ten-year-olds uncensored access to the internet? When would they countenance drinking, drugs, sex?

Parzival's departure from Soltane triggers a series of consequences that, in his childlike innocence, he cannot entirely comprehend. Unbeknownst to him, his mother dies from a broken heart just after he leaves. He blithely sets off in search of knighthood, but he acts in a decidedly unknightly fashion when he intrudes upon a sleeping lady and steals an embrace, a brooch, and a bellyful of food from her. He then stumbles upon the lovely Sigune, mourning her beloved Schianatulander, who lies dead in her lap. At key junctures in the story she will appear to give Parzival new pieces of self-knowledge, even as she draws ever closer to joining her beloved in death. Here she reveals his actual name to him, which she says means "right through the middle,"[64] as well as his royal lineage and his kinship to Sigune.

Later, when confronted by a knight all dressed in red, Parzival kills him just because he desires his armor. Now on horseback and wearing another knight's "identity," Parzival ends up at the castle of Gurnemanz, who trains him in all the exoteric knowledge Parzival never learned before about knighthood, from skills in combat to simple courtesies. Among the advice Gurnemanz dispenses to the young Parzival, none looms larger than the admonition, "Do not ask too many questions."[65]

Parzival departs once again, and quickly puts his newly-acquired training to use. In a scenario eerily reminiscent of his father's destiny, he liberates a besieged queen and her kingdom, then falls deeply in love with Condwiramurs. They marry, he becomes a king and, if this were a standard fairy tale, the story would end here, with the assurance that they would live happily ever after. However, *Parzival* is no typical story; in fact, von Eschenbach is barely one quarter of the way through his tale. He clearly has another aim in mind. Parzival has mastered the art of knighthood easily enough—too easily—but the art of *selfhood* has eluded him thus far. All of his exploits up to this point serve as a mere prologue to his true quest.

When Parzival's inherited restlessness impels him to leave his new wife and go in search of his mother, the story shifts into a bizarre and unfamiliar realm. Parzival finds himself in a castle called Munsalvaesche, hosted by a grievously wounded knight named Anfortas and inhabited by four hundred mournful knights. During a mysterious ceremony, Parzival watches as a squire comes into the hall bearing a lance with blood gushing from its point. Then a procession of maidens enters, one of whom carries the Grail, which is described only as "the perfection of paradise."[66] Whatever one desires to eat or drink, the Grail provides. Parzival is then given the gift of an exquisite sword, "whose edges run exactly parallel to each other."[67] (One student noted that parallel lines meet in infinity—a detail that adds resonance to the spiritual nature of this entire experience at Munsalvaesche.) Through all of these extraordinary events, Parzival neglects to ask a single question. He goes to his room, endures nightmarish dreams, and awakens to a deserted castle.

Later, at the court of King Arthur, just as he is about to be welcomed into the brotherhood of the Round Table, an unspeakably ugly figure appears. Cundrie *la sorciere* had

> a nose like a dog's, and two boar's teeth stuck out from her mouth. Cundrie had ears like a bear's and no lover

could desire a face like hers, hairy and rough...and the hands of this charming dear looked like a monkey's skin.[68]

She proceeds to curse Parzival for not asking the question that would have healed his host at Munsalvaesche. Students often have strong reactions to this turning point in the story. They wonder about the significance of Cundrie's beastly appearance. Many question the severity of her tirade. Cundrie apparently holds Parzival responsible for not knowing what to say and do at the Grail castle; and yet, they argue, what could have possibly prepared him for such an encounter? Furthermore, what good does it do to publicly shame him? Finally, students are generally baffled by the unexpected twist the story takes at Munsalvaesche. Based on Cundrie's denunciation, Parzival has just failed the most important test of his life. What does that failure portend? Each of these concerns deserves attention. Regarding Cundrie's appearance, one student proposed that her ugly exterior might be a reflection of something unattractive in Parzival's interior.

Figure 8 – Classwork during Parzival *main lesson*

After all, to this point, for all his knightly courtesies, he seems rather superficial, callow and self-absorbed. Indeed, such outer/inner correspondences occur throughout the book. For example, just as he is leaving Munsalvaesche, a squire calls after him, "You are a goose. If you had only moved your jaws and asked your host the question!"[69] Then shortly thereafter, Parzival sees a falcon attack and wound a goose. The deserted Grail castle to which he awakens certainly suggests Parzival's sudden feeling of abandonment and aloneness. One of Parzival's "handicaps" is his inability to recognize the correspondences between outer circumstances and inner soul conditions.

The question of Parzival's accountability is a fascinating one. Students often argue whether Parzival should be held responsible for his failure to ask the proper question at the Grail castle. "He was just following Gurnemanz's advice not to ask too many questions," asserts one. "Look," says another, "If someone advises you to run a red light and you do it, who pays the fine—you or your advisor?" Usually, eleventh graders eventually agree that Parzival committed a mistake that we all make all the time; he misguidedly relied on lessons from the past in confronting the present. He tried to apply earthly advice to what we might call a spiritual experience at Munsalvaesche. His failure stems from not yet possessing the presence of mind to act appropriately in the moment.

One of the most important lessons for young people is that Parzival initially fails. Failure has gotten a bad reputation in our culture. Nobody wants to fail. Most of us go to great lengths to avoid failure, because it calls into question our amazingly fragile sense of ourselves, our self-esteem. Failure breeds doubt; yet if the doubt begets a genuine questioning—and every question contains a quest—then failure can be the catalyst that brings our greatest moments of growth.

After Cundrie's shaming, for the first time in his life, Parzival is tormented by doubt, the plague of clear, purposeful thinking. He even questions his relationship to God, who appears to have abandoned him in Parzival's darkest hour.

> Alas, what is God? If He were mighty, if God could rule with power, He would never have imposed such disgrace. I was in His service since I hoped to receive His grace. But now I shall renounce His service, and if He hates me, that hate I will bear.[70]

At the same time he resolves "to allow myself no joy until I have seen the Grail, be the time short or long."[71] His pledge to redeem himself by finding again the Grail castle becomes his all-consuming aim.

Figure 8 – Classwork during Parzival *main lesson*

A few years ago I came across a poem by a man named Albert Huffstickler called "The Edge of Doubt." It expresses the virtues of uncertainty in a distinctively modern voice.

> There's always that edge of doubt.
> Trust it. That's where
> the new things come from. If
> you can't live with it, get out,
> because when it's gone
> you're on automatic,
> repeating something you've learned.

> Let your prayer be:
> Save me from that tempting
> certainty that leads me back
> from the edge, that dark edge where
> the first light breaks.[72]

Eleventh graders experience first-hand that doubt can become the driving force in their lives to seek for the light of truth, just as it is in Parzival's case. His doubt arises from a fracture in the foundations upon which he has built his life, and this fracture widens to open a space in his soul for a new knowlege, this time from a hermit who turns out to be Parzival's uncle. Trevrizent teaches Parzival about the origins of humanity and of the Grail, about his own lineage, about forgiveness. However, it takes Parzival years to overcome his soul wound. When he finally does transform himself after years of suffering, isolation and loneliness, regains faith in God, develops empathy for others, and elevates his thinking—only then does Cundrie reappear to declare his impending kingship of the Grail.

It should be noted that she returns only after two near catastrophes. Inadvertently Parzival nearly vanquishes his valiant friend, Sir Gawain, in a joust. Gawain assumes a central role, appropriately enough, in the "heart" of the book. His quest has veered away from the search for the Grail and now leads him through a bizarre, parallel universe interpenetrating Parzival's, wherein Gawain seems destined to purify the murky domain of feelings. Instead of freeing the four hundred knights in the Grail castle from their misery, he finds that his mission is to liberate four hundred ladies held captive in the Castle of Wonders. While Parzival receives a sword at the castle, Gawain receives a shield before he enters. Instead of simply using words to heal the Grail king and his kingdom, Gawain must rely upon his courage to survive the treacherous Wonder Bed, then use his sword to conquer a monstrous lion. While Parzival is beset by the gravest of doubts, Gawain must endure being the object of doubt.

Figure 9 – Classwork during Parzival *main lesson*

Some students question Gawain's relevance to Parzival's story, but their more perceptive classmates recognize the close connection of the two knights' adventures. Von Eschenbach himself makes the link clear when Gawain is nearly defeated by a mysterious knight who, of course, turns out to be Parzival. When Parzival realizes that he has exchanged blows with a kinsman and friend, he cries out, "It is myself I have vanquished," a thought echoed by Gawain: "Your hand gained the victory over us both, now may you grieve for the sake of us both. It is yourself you have vanquished."[73] On some metaphorical level, Gawain is a part of Parzival. Parzival now incorporates all that Gawain has won in the realm of relationships, as the two streams become one.

The other near-catastrophe occurs when Parzival does battle with yet another stranger, who quickly proves himself the most formidable foe Parzival has ever faced. On the verge of losing his first hand-to-hand combat ever to this mighty warrior, Parzival breaks his sword; instead of pressing his advantage, his opponent stops the clash so that the combatants can identify themselves.

Here von Eschenbach weaves the last remaining strand back into the fabric of his story, for the stranger turns out to be none other than Parzival's half-brother Feirefiz from the Moorish East, the son of Gahmuret and Belacane. Because of his parents' union, Feirefiz "bears the markings of the magpie"[74]—he is spotted black and white. The brothers' embrace signifies yet another merging of soul capacities—Feirefiz's indomitable will forces meld with Parzival's refined thinking capacities and Gawain's mastery over the feeling life. Only now, endowed with newly developed powers of thinking, feeling and willing, is Parzival ready to become the Lord of the Grail.

Eleventh graders certainly recognize the significance of integrating these thinking, feeling and willing faculties in their own lives. They often act out the disconnectedness they feel between their thoughts and their feelings, or between their thoughts and their will. One young woman will stand back and coolly, even cruelly, criticize her teachers and classmates; her thinking needs to be warmed up by her feelings. A classmate of hers has the bad habit of idly carving on desktops; he must be reminded to not act so impulsively, to bring more consciousness to his will. Yet another junior will flare up fervently in class over the smallest perceived slight; she, too, needs to bring more objective observation and reflection to her interactions.

Rudolf Steiner predicted that at the end of the twentieth century forces in the world would intensify to separate these three capacities, to "dis-integrate" them. We can see how across the globe, blind, brutal will hacks out a swath of thoughtless destruction, while in skull-shaped legislative chambers, calculating politicians create intellectual constructs remarkably devoid of positive action. The resurgence of religious fanaticism shows just how ruinous unbridled passions (or worse yet, passions yoked to ungoverned will impulses) can be. By the end of *Parzival*, von Eschenbach has given us a prototype of thinking, feeling and willing reunited and integrated in an enlightened individual.

Interestingly, when Cundrie reappears to proclaim Parzival's imminent reign as Lord of the Grail, she also includes a stipulation: he cannot return to the Grail Castle alone; he must bring someone with him. Appropriately, Parzival chooses his brother Feirefiz, representative of the East. Consider the implications for eleventh graders who read Cundrie's stated condition. They are in the middle of a stage of life where self-absorption and self-interest are almost considered entitlements. Yet the end of *Parzival* suggests that our greatest destiny moments cannot be accomplished by or for ourselves. We must bring our brothers and sisters with us. Furthermore, if we stop doing battle with our perceived foes long enough to actually engage them in conversation, as Parzival and Feirefiz manage to do, then we, too, might recognize our hidden kinship. What a novel idea to apply to all those persistent conflicts that afflict humanity in East and West—in the crucibles of the Middle East, Africa, Ireland, Kashmir, Chechnya, the Balkans.

So Parzival returns with his brother to Munsalvaesche and succeeds where he had once failed. He finally inquires of the wounded Anfortas, "Uncle, what ails thee?"[75]—the question that can only be asked out of an abiding interest in "the other." The moment he does so, Anfortas is healed and the kingdom restored. The former knight of the Sword has become the knight of the Word.

In *Hamlet*, eleventh graders read of yet another ailing kingdom and another noble prince caught between swords and words. However, unlike Parzival, Hamlet cannot overcome his own isolation or summon the forces to purge Elsinore of its toxicity.

Hamlet: The First Modern Individual

Today's youth know *Hamlet*, even before they read a word of the play. Perhaps they have seen one of the many stage revivals constantly being performed around the world; perhaps they have watched some cinematic version—older classics starring Laurence Olivier or Richard Burton, or one of the newer films that have appeared in the past few years, with Mel Gibson or Kenneth

Branaugh or Ethan Hawke in the title role. Yet even if they have managed to avoid the movie glut, young people know *Hamlet* the way that indigenous tribes once intuitively knew nature. Nature taught those people living in its bosom which plants were medicinal and which were poisonous, which animals to trap and which to avoid, where to set up camp and how to stay warm. *Hamlet* has had a similar effect on our culture by teaching us about our own modern consciousness, this double-edged sword that allows us to understand the world even as it separates us from it.

Of course, *Hamlet*'s influence in today's world is ubiquitous. Snippets of memorable lines from the play find their way into everyday conversations: "The play's the thing"; "Frailty, thy name is woman"; "Brevity is the soul of wit"; "Something is rotten in the state of Denmark"; "Methinks the lady doth protest too much"; "Sweets to the sweet"; and, of course, the now iconic "To be or not to be." Hundreds of book titles have been spawned by the play's exquisite language. However, memorable language alone has not turned *Hamlet* into a modern-day obsession, nor is it the reason that Waldorf students around the world read the play in eleventh grade. That has more to do with the nature of Hamlet's dilemma and how he thinks ... and thinks, and thinks some more about it.

The predicament, of course, stems from Hamlet's conflicting feelings. He finds himself trapped between a directive charging him to avenge his father's death and his newly emerging, modern consciousness that seeks a rational basis for every action. The students nearly always resonate with Hamlet's dilemma, especially those who have begun to experience the existential conundrum of life itself—the "To be or not to be" question—or those who have had to make some excruciating decision that seems to have no absolutely right answer.

Part of Hamlet's problem has to do with the world in which he lives. Elsinore seems a god-forsaken kingdom (one possible etymology of the word: *El* = Hebrew for *God*, *sine* = Latin for *without*), where treachery infects the very atmosphere. The first scene begins with jittery sentries fearful that they will once again behold the ghost of the recently departed King Hamlet. Hamlet the son's encounter with the ghost leaves him with a seemingly clear course of action: kill the villainous uncle, Claudius, who poisoned Hamlet's father while he was sleeping in his garden and who then married Hamlet's mother before her former husband "was two months dead."[76] However, while he pledges to sweep to his revenge "with wings as swift as meditation or the thoughts of love,"[77] his plan bogs down in a series of musings. He questions his own courage:

> O, what a rogue and peasant slave am I...
> It cannot be
> But I am pigeon-liver'd and lack gall
> To make oppression bitter, or ere this
> I should have fatted all the region kites
> With this slave's offal.[78]

He begins to doubt the authenticity of the ghost: "The spirit that I have seen/may be a devil; and the devil hath power/T' assume a pleasing shape."[79]

Yet, despite his misgivings and indecisiveness, Hamlet is no fool. On the contrary, he is preternaturally perceptive. He sees the cesspool of scheming that Claudius and Polonius create; He treats them and their henchmen, Rosenkrantz and Guildenstern, as he would "adders fanged."[80] He knows he is being watched and resolves to be a wilier watcher. This tactic leads to one of the most significant scenes in all of Shakespeare's plays: the play within the play, whereby Hamlet hopes to "catch the conscience of the king."[81]

When the king and queen and their entourage assemble to view *The Murder of Gonzago*, students can sense the ironies multiplying, and not only because the usurping king witnesses a clever reenactment of his own murderous deed. While the audience watches the play, Hamlet and Horatio are carefully eyeing Claudius for any telltale signs of guilt. Of course, at the same time Hamlet is under surveillance by Polonius, Rosenkrantz and Guildenstern. Meanwhile, we who are attending the performance of *Hamlet* comprise yet another audience watching the watchers watching one another. One eleventh grader took these concentric circles one step further, reminding us that there is one other witness to the unfolding events—the ghost.

The magnitude of this scene becomes more apparent within the larger context of history. Inspired by Rudolf Steiner's description of the evolution of human consciousness, Owen Barfield often writes about the vast difference in awareness between ancient and modern people. The former possessed what he terms "participatory consciousness." They lived in a state of oneness with their surroundings and experienced little separation between the outer world and their own inner lives. Eleventh graders have cited parallels between this early condition of humanity and the development of individual human beings. The students point to their own early childhoods as an example of this undivided experience. They can vaguely remember when they felt no space between themselves and the moon, when time had no meaning because it slipped by unnoticed in the continual pleasures of the moment.

Barfield suggests that, over time, humanity has slowly lost this participatory feeling and in its stead, a new capacity has emerged that enables us to live in the material world ever more concretely, even as a veil has been drawn over the spiritual realities so transparent to the ancients. The cost for these cognitive capacities has been nothing less than our most primal sense of belonging. Starting with adolescence, we experience the duality of life, of our own, separated selves *in here* and the world *out there*, with a seemingly unbridgeable gulf in between. We have become spectators to our own lives, a truth that reaches hyperbolic proportions whenever we see people "enjoying" their vacations or weddings through the lens of a video camera.

In *Hamlet*, Shakespeare intensifies this "spectator consciousness" to an almost unbearable degree. We see the consequences of living in a world where individuals are so isolated that they mistrust, deceive, and are ultimately cut off from one another. Nearly every relationship is a sham. Except for his friendship with Horatio, who is the only major character to survive the carnage of the last scene, all Hamlet's interactions bear bitter fruit. Ophelia is his heart's desire, yet she is merely an obedient pawn in her father's intrigues and ultimately betrays Hamlet. Ophelia, too, is torn between two incompatible impulses, between dutiful, medieval daughter on the one hand and independent agent upholding her own sense of integrity on the other. Unfortunately, Ophelia lacks enough sense of her own self to withstand the treachery poisoning Elsinore, so when her would-be lover kills her intrusive father, she loses her moorings and goes mad.

Madness—real and feigned—colors much of the action in *Hamlet* and occupies much of the students' attention. Some eleventh graders suggest that madness may be the only truly protective response to living in such an insidious world. They understand Ophelia's descent into insanity even as they criticize her for being too weak-willed and compliant. Hamlet's "madness" is another matter. Do we take him at his word when, before the final, fatal duel, he asks Laertes' forgiveness for his outrageous actions at Ophelia's graveside?

> You must needs have heard, how I am punished
> With sore distraction. What I have done
> That might your nature, honor and exception
> Roughly awake, I here proclaim was madness.
> Was 't Hamlet wronged Laertes? Never Hamlet.
> If Hamlet from himself be ta'en away,
> And when he's not himself does wrong Laertes,
> Then Hamlet does it not, Hamlet denies it.
> Who does it, then? His madness. If 't be so,
> Hamlet is of the faction that is wronged:
> His madness is poor Hamlet's enemy.[82]

Or do we rather believe him when he confides to Rosenkrantz and Guildenstern, "I am but mad north-north-west. When the wind is southerly, I know a hawk from a handsaw"?[83] The first is an acknowledgement—and a brilliant defense—of the temporary insanity plea; the second an admission that Hamlet's "sore distraction" is pure, premeditated pretense. By the end, most students can live with the paradox of both statements bearing truth. While Hamlet can be astoundingly devious in his dealings with Polonius, Claudius, Rosenkrantz and Guildenstern, he also loses himself several times during the play. This occurs most notably during the "Get thee to a nunnery" tirade directed at Ophelia, again in his mother's bedchamber when she actually fears for her life, and a third time when grappling with Laertes in Ophelia's grave.

Yet he also seems strikingly self-possessed during the rest of Act V. With remarkable equanimity, he anticipates and accepts the inevitability of his death.

> We defy augury: there's a special providence in the fall
> of a sparrow. If it be now, 'tis not to come. If it be not
> to come, it will be now; if it be not now, yet it will come;
> the readiness is all.[84]

In the gravedigger scene, he also ruminates profoundly about death as he holds Yorick's skull.

> Not one now, to mock your own grinning? Quite
> chapfall'n? Now get you to my lady's chamber, and
> tell her, let her paint an inch think, to this favor she
> must come....Dost thou think Alexander looked o' this
> fashion i' the earth? ....Alexander died, Alexander was
> buried, Alexander returneth into dust; the dust is earth;
> of earth we make loam; and why of that loam (whereto
> he was converted) might they not stop a beer barrel?[85]

Hamlet's meditations on death are hardly the ravings of a lunatic. On the contrary, they comprise some of the most probing commentary ever written about our fascination with mortality. It is also telling that on several occasions Hamlet links dying to dust in the above passage and again in his famous "What a piece of work is man" speech extolling the divine virtues of the human being, which he ends with the deflating words, "And yet, to me, what is this quintessence of dust?"[86]

Perhaps it should not surprise us that Hamlet is so preoccupied with the connection between death and dust. After all, this spectator consciousness seems to be inextricably bound to the material plane. The further we drift away from our spiritual ancestry, the more earthbound our thinking becomes. It becomes a wonderful tool for plumbing the secrets of the material world, as natural scientists have been doing for the past six hundred years. However, without that higher guidance, it also isolates us from one another and from the very world we want to investigate.

Ultimately, Hamlet is not a play about revenge, or treachery, or madness; it is about the emergence of a new consciousness, not just in one individual, but in all individuals. Some eleventh graders identify with Hamlet more than any other character they meet in the junior year. Despite the play's being over four hundred years old, Hamlet sees the world through the same contemporary, self-

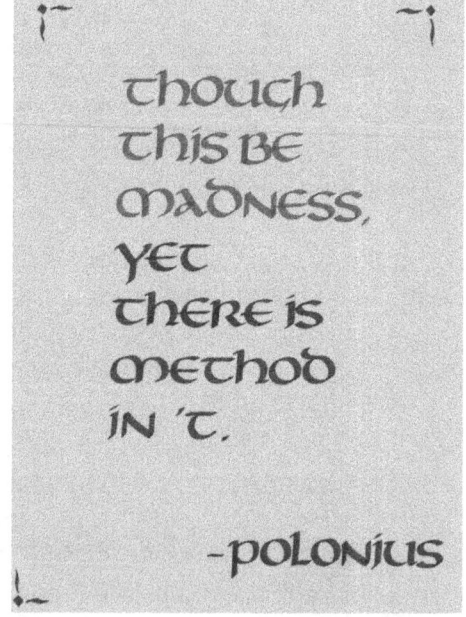

Figure 10 – Calligraphy classwork during Shakespeare *main lesson*

conscious eyes as they do. He broods over the same questions they carry about the purpose of living, the meaning of dying, the mystery of what lies beyond the threshold of death. They recognize that they are all Hamlets, no longer able to simply abide by the commands or dictates of past ghosts. They find themselves left largely to their own devices, "crawling between heaven and earth."[87] Like Hamlet they are all looking for terra firma—a little island perhaps, rising out of the turbulent seas—on which they can stand and act out of freely chosen initiative. Shakespeare gives them that island in his last, enchanted play, *The Tempest*.

The Tempest: Virtue Rather than Vengeance

Eleventh graders don't need to mull over the shattering finale of Hamlet for very long. It is enough that they have experienced a murder before the action even begins, a supernatural encounter with an apparition, possible adultery, a young woman going insane, wrestling in a grave, and no fewer than eight deaths. At the play's end, the stage is littered with the corpses of Claudius, Gertrude, Hamlet and Laertes. Despite Hamlet's noble soul, it appears that the forces of darkness have been too overpowering for him to purge Elsinore of its poison. While students can feel elevated simply from witnessing Hamlet struggle against odds, they can also feel some of his despair over "how weary, stale, flat and unprofitable/Seem to me all the uses of the world."[88]

Shakespeare's final work—*The Tempest*—can provide a welcome balm for juniors' unsettled souls. As in *Hamlet*, treachery precedes and casts a shadow over the initial action. Prospero, rightful Duke of Milan, has been overthrown by his brother Alonso. Prospero is not entirely blameless here, for he has largely neglected the affairs of state to pursue magical arts. He and his infant daughter Miranda have been left to perish in an unseaworthy vessel, but Providence intervenes. Father and daughter end up on an island, where Prospero acquires two servants. One is an airy sprite named Ariel, now indentured to Prospero for his freeing the elemental being from a tree trunk. The other is Caliban, foul, subhuman offspring of a witch, and whom Prospero raised most lovingly until he "didst seek to violate the honor of my child."[89]

Prospero has used the years well, caring for the lovely Miranda as she reaches adolescence, and deepening his knowledge of magic. His powers have become so potent that he raises a tempest for the purpose of bringing the ship carrying his usurping brother and accomplices to his island. When students hear Prospero unfold to Miranda the egregious plot against him, they fear that they will have to witness yet another finale filled with carnage. However, Prospero has instructed Ariel that all aboard the ship carrying the conspirators should reach land unharmed.

Early in the play, students begin to suspect that this locale is no ordinary island and that the story is no typical tale of revenge. Shakespeare peoples this island not only with villains, but with two drunken fools, Stephano and Trinculo, and a Prince Charming for Miranda—young Ferdinand, son of the usurping Duke, who the survivors believe has drowned in the tempest. The besotted twosome stumble upon Caliban, introduce him to the excesses of intoxication, and join him in a daft, doomed plot to overthrow Prospero. At the same time, Prospero orchestrates a meeting between Ferdinand and Miranda, who immediately fall in love. Yet Prospero treats Ferdinand roughly, despite Miranda's protestations that "There's nothing ill can dwell in such a temple."[90] Prospero understands that "This swift business/I must uneasy make, lest too light winning/Make the prize light."[91]

While, on the one hand, Prospero plays matchmaker and, on the other, punishes the inebriated trio of plotters, he relies on Ariel to create a kind of purgatory for the real conspirators. The sprite appears as a harpy; however, instead of tearing them limb from limb as Dante's harpies do in the Wood of the Suicides, Ariel turns their eyes inward to behold their stained souls. Some sharp eleventh graders will hark back to Hamlet's confrontation with his mother in the bedchamber scene, when his words "like daggers" entered her ears and "turn'st mine eyes into my very soul,/And there I see such black and grained spots/As will not leave their tinct."[92]

Ariel provides an even more harrowing mirror into which the usurping Duke and company must gaze:

> Ye are three men of sin, whom Destiny,
> That hath to instrument this lower world
> And what is in 't, the never-surfeited sea
> Hath caused to belch up you. ...But remember
> For that's my business to you—that you three
> From Milan did supplant good Prospero,
> Exposed unto the sea, which hath requit it,
> Him and his innocent child, for which foul deed...
> Ling'ring perdition, worse than any death
> Shall step by step attend you and your ways,
> Whose wrath to guard you from...is nothing
> But heart's sorrow and a clear life ensuing.[93]

In a classical tragedy, this moment of recognition might well be followed by the deaths of the villains and of Prospero and Miranda too. Cordelia's cruel death in *King Lear* reminds us that not even Miranda's innocence would save her from such a fate. Thankfully, this is not a tragedy, but a romance, in which the shadowy threat of death or loss is always counterbalanced by the redeeming power of love.

At the climactic moment of the play, Ariel describes to her master how the conspirators remain imprisoned and "brimful of sorrow and dismay.../Your charm so strongly works 'em/That if you now beheld them, your affections/Would become tender."[94] Prospero now takes a step that few mortals ever manage. He embraces the notion of forgiveness.

> And mine shall.
> Hast thou, which are but air, a touch, a feeling

> Of their afflictions, and shall not myself,
> One of their kind, that relish all as sharply
> Passion as they, be kindlier moved than thou art?
> Though with their high wrong I am struck to th' quick
> Yet with my nobler reason 'gainst my fury
> Do I take part. The rarer action is
> In virtue than in vengeance. They being penitent,
> The sole drift of my purpose doth extend
> Not a frown further. Go, release them Ariel.
> My charms I'll break, their senses I'll restore,
> And they shall be themselves.[95]

Due either to external circumstances or to some constitutional deficiency, Hamlet could not reach this lofty plane. Students certainly recognize Prospero as a more developed individual than Hamlet, but, perhaps not surprisingly, they have a harder time relating to him than to Hamlet. Hamlet is as much a suffering soul as they are, just as tortured by his limitations and acutely aware of his possibilities. He may be as insightful as Prospero, but he lacks the mastery over his own nature, much less over the forces of nature, to choose "the rarer action." Prospero possesses faculties so evolved that he seems more Olympian than mortal, more faultless than flawed.

Occasionally, a particularly astute class will want to go more deeply into the possible meanings of the play. What do Prospero and Ariel and Caliban really represent? What about the island itself? The young lovers?

By the spring of eleventh grade, students are familiar with one approach that considers the various characters in a story as aspects of a single human being. Seen in this light, the image of the island might support the notion that each of us living in this modern age is an entity unto ourselves. We are all surrounded by waters—some more shark-infested than others—looking for ways to build bridges to neighboring islands.

Based on his powers, Prospero seems to exemplify some "higher self." However, students like to point out that he is not perfect; by raising the storm, he has exploited nature for his own purposes. He has used his charms to intrude upon others' free will. One of his spells puts Miranda to sleep, and another consigns Ferdinand to hauling logs. Prospero as much as admits his shortcomings when he introduces Caliban to the now repentant, shipwrecked party. "This thing of darkness I/Acknowledge mine."[96] Caliban is one of Shakespeare's most original and, paradoxically, archetypal creations. Coarse, cursing and mutinous, Caliban bridles under Prospero's control (in Sanskrit, "Kali" is another name for Devi, dark goddess of death and destruction; it also means strife, discord, quarrel); in Caliban's eyes, Prospero is the usurper, having displaced the son of a witch from his reign over the island as sovereign and sole inhabitant. Caliban would like nothing more than to "knock a nail" into Prospero's head. When his ludicrous scheme is foiled, he promises to "be wise hereafter/And seek for grace."[97]

Some students have contended validly that if Prospero represents a higher ego, then Caliban is his lower, unredeemed self, constantly needing to be restrained by the self-possessed ego strength of the former. Without that vigilant "overseer," Caliban reels from volcanic feelings to reckless actions. Young people for whom impulse control is a daily battle are well acquainted with this "Caliban" within them. He is the creature of instinct, constantly cooking up plots to wrest control away from the more prudent, far-sighted Prospero-ego. Some students inwardly grimace with recognition at the idiocy that results when Caliban's rashness is "lubricated" by Stephano's and Trinculo's alcohol.

Ariel offers a striking contrast to the dense, subearthly Caliban. Ariel is a being of air and light. As a spirit-servant, Ariel executes Prospero's wishes to the letter. Except for a moment or two when Prospero upbraids Ariel for demanding prematurely to be emancipated, master and servant are in accord. Ariel is the perfect shape-shifter—one moment "flaming amazement" aboard the traitors' ship, the next invisibly drawing Ferdinand towards Miranda with enchanting melodies, and then soon after appearing as the harpy who shakes the conspirators' souls into confronting their misdeeds. Ariel seems to act as some refined organ of Prospero's own being, like Caliban, connected to the will, but a higher, enlightened version that transforms Prospero's thoughts into realities.

We cannot forget that it is Ariel who turns into the "teacher" at the play's climax, nudging Prospero away from revenge and towards forgiveness. After Ariel describes the pitiful condition of the conspirators and gently suggests his feelings might turn tender, Prospero asks, "Does thou think so, spirit?" Ariel replies, "Mine would, sir, were I human."[98] Indeed, Ariel is more than human—superhuman, in the same sense that Caliban is subhuman. Shakespeare seems to be gently reminding us that we must rise above Caliban's primitive impulsiveness as we strive to rise towards Ariel's spirit-filled will.

Students are often baffled by Prospero's surrendering of his magical powers at the play's end. They cannot understand why he would give up the "art" he has spent a lifetime mastering. "It would be like Picasso throwing away his brush, or YoYo Ma his bow, at the height of his powers," said one junior. Hopefully what becomes clear to them by the end of the play is that Prospero understands the true meaning of freedom. He has bent nature to his will.

> I have bedimmed
> The noontide sun, called forth the mutinous winds
> And 'twixt the green sea and the azured vault
> Set roaring roar; to the dread rattling thunder
> Have I given fire, and rifted Jove's stout oak
> With his own bolt.[99]

Once he has achieved his aims—the contrition of the conspirators and the union of Ferdinand and Miranda—he needs to liberate Ariel and the entire elemental world from his control. He pledges that

> This rough magic
> I here abjure, and when I have required
> Some heavenly music, which even now I do,
> To work mine end upon their senses that
> This airy charm is for, I'll break my staff,
> Bury it certain fathoms in the earth,
> And deeper than did ever plummet sound
> I'll drown my book.[100]

These actions do not free only his servants. Prospero has spent all of his years on the island living in a cave that he calls "his cell." By emancipating Ariel and then renouncing his magic, Prospero is also freeing himself from his dependence upon supernatural powers. It is as if he epitomizes the sacrifice that all of humanity has made in gradually losing touch with the direct spiritual guidance of the past. In the epilogue, when he addresses the audience, Prospero speaks both to, and on behalf of, all of us:

> Now my charms are all overthrown
> And what strength I have 's mine own.
> Now I want
> Spirits to enforce, art to enchant,
> And my ending is despair,
> Unless I be relieved by prayer,
> Which pierces so that it assaults
> Mercy itself, and frees all faults.[101]

He has learned the lesson of compassion and asks no less from us—students and teachers alike—so that we, too, might experience what it means to be truly human.

The Romantic Poets: Seeing into the Life of Things

Years ago when I was in high school, I remember panicking over a literature assignment. I had no idea what to write about. A veteran senior came to my rescue when she advised, "It doesn't matter what the book's about. You can always write about one of three themes: the individual's relationship to God, to other people, or to nature." Forty years later, her words still ring true. In *The Tempest*, nature is omnipresent; except for the final scene when Ferdinand and Miranda are discovered in Prospero's cave playing chess, the entire play is enacted in the enchanted, open air of the isle. Furthermore, nature is subservient to the will of a man who uses nature to so transform evildoers that they can once again be their authentic selves, "when no man was his own."[102]

In *Hamlet*, the play takes place largely inside the suffocating, menacing air of Elsinore. When the characters do venture outside the castle walls, they encounter a ghost (as do Hamlet and the sentries), embark on a sea voyage that is a prelude to execution (for Rosenkrantz and Guildenstern), end up grappling in a grave (Hamlet and Laertes) or drown (Ophelia). Far from possessing the restorative power that it has in *The Tempest*, nature in *Hamlet* continually brings us face-to-face with the inescapable fact of death. And yet, one can sense in Hamlet his desperate longing to escape the toxic atmosphere, to find some safe and tranquil setting that will heal his wounded soul and restore his broken world.

Teenagers today have a similar longing. Nearly eighty years ago Rudolf Steiner spoke to an audience of young people. "Where there sounds the call for nature, it arises out of the youth-filled soul, desiring to have a memory, a unification with the divine source of everything."[103]

Historically, this yearning can be traced back to the late eighteenth century, specifically to the groundbreaking art of the English Romantic poets. William Wordsworth and Samuel Taylor Coleridge were born into the Age of Revolution, in 1770 and 1772, respectively. In the American colonies and in France, one could hear the rumblings of subjugated peoples desperate to throw off the yoke of oppression. On both sides of the Atlantic, yearnings for liberty, equality and fraternity started to stir. At the same time, the

Industrial Revolution was already beginning to alter human beings' relationship to the natural world. For centuries, people had lived in rural settings, partnering with nature to produce life's necessities. Country folks may have lacked luxuries, but they experienced a certain social and economic wholeness on their farms and homesteads. They were usually involved in the entire process of production. For example, one could trace the knitting of a sweater back to each step of its creation, from pasturing and shearing the sheep, to carding, dyeing and spinning the wool.

Waldorf students are well-acquainted with the consequences of the invention of steam-powered machines. Within a generation or two, cottage industry virtually disappeared, supplanted by the factories and mills that sprang up in urban areas. Unable to compete with cheap, manufactured products, people streamed into the teeming cities to create the work force that operated the factories. Some got rich, some lived in appallingly impoverished conditions, but all lived lives more isolated from nature than ever before.

Even though he spent much of his life in the bucolic Lake District of Northwestern England, Wordsworth was acutely aware of this seismic shift in human lives.

> The world is too much with us: late and soon,
> Getting and spending, we lay waste our powers;
> Little we see in Nature that is ours;
> We have given our hearts away, a sordid boon![104]

Early in his career, he saw the dire effects for the human soul of this dislocating industrialization. Yet the Industrial Revolution was as much a consequence as it was a cause of this human estrangement from nature. The moment individuals began to step back from the natural world and to perceive it as separate from themselves, the seeds were sown for this alienation. Like the preenlightened Prospero, we learned to subjugate nature for our own ends.

Wordsworth and Coleridge wanted to bridge the growing divide between the self and the realm of nature. They were bold enough to announce their intentions in the preface to their slim volume of poems, first published in 1798 and unassumingly titled *Lyrical Ballads, with a Few Other Poems.* Students are often taken aback by the self-conscious tone of the preface. In it, Wordsworth proposed nothing less than to chart a new direction in poetry, and that is exactly what he and Coleridge achieved. Before the appearance of *Lyrical Ballads*, poetry had become largely a diverting entertainment, shaped by wit and artifice. Alexander Pope's "The Rape of the Lock" was the much-admired Neo-Classical ideal, amusing its audience as a mock epic about a salon party, during which a gentleman surreptitiously cuts off a lock of an unsuspecting lady's hair.

Romanticism arose in large measure as a protest against the superficiality and pretense of this Neo-Classical poetry. In the preface, Wordsworth enumerated the ingredients for this new poetry. It would focus on "incidents and situations from common life...in language really used by men."[105] Furthermore, it would embody the belief that "the passions of men are incorporated with the beautiful and permanent forms of nature."[106] It would also have a worthy purpose, as opposed to the capricious and trivial poetry of the past that seemed designed only to "furnish food for fickle tastes."[107] Perhaps most famously, Wordsworth described this new poetry as "the spontaneous overflow of powerful feelings.[108]

Spontaneity-loving juniors often stop at this juncture to applaud Wordsworth's characterization; it seems to validate their own emotional outpourings on paper, which they then call poetry and jealously defend against the critical comments of unsympathetic English teachers. Critiquing student poetry is always a delicate task, especially when dealing with young people who believe that the words on the page are the outer expression of their very tender and exposed feelings. Offering even the slightest constructive criticism that suggests they revise their work can be construed as a brutal attack on their very souls. Thankfully, Wordsworth goes on to add a crucial stipulation to his oft-quoted line above.

> For all good poetry is the spontaneous overflow of powerful feelings: but though this be true, poems to which any value can be attached, were never produced on any variety of subjects but by a man, who being possessed of more than usual organic sensibility, *had also thought long and deeply.*[109]
> [italics inserted by author]

Thus, eleventh graders discover, sadly enough, that they cannot indiscriminately cite Wordsworth as an exponent of that popular adolescent, stream-of-consciousness approach to poetry.

Some students can, however, relate to his worshipful regard for nature. Wordsworth was not the first poet to venerate the natural world; we can find countless examples of nature's celebrated status in virtually every indigenous literature around the world. Yet Wordsworth and the other Romantic poets added a new dimension to this reverence for nature. Never before had human beings experienced their subjective selves so divided from nature; never before had they felt so keenly the need to bridge the chasm that divided their stunted, mortal souls from nature's eternal wellsprings. They looked to nature not just as soothing balm or revitalizing agent. For the Romantics, nature was nothing less than an expression of the creative, divine force that could help human beings reclaim their sense of oneness with the world. As Wordsworth writes in "Tintern Abbey,"

> And I have felt
> A presence that disturbs me with the joy
> Of elevated thoughts; a sense sublime
> Of something far more deeply interfused
> Whose dwelling is the light of setting suns,

> And the round ocean and the living air,
> And the blue sky, and in the mind of man:
> A motion and a spirit that impels
> All thinking things, all objects of all thought,
> And rolls through all things.[110]

Eleventh graders may not believe that nature is the handiwork of the gods; indeed, many teenagers at this age are just entering a nihilistic phase that denies the existence of any higher power. Yet it does not escape their notice when Wordsworth ascribes to nature an almost mystical capacity to elevate human morality:

> feelings too
> of unremembered pleasure: such perhaps,
> As have no slight or trivial influence
> On that best portion of a good man's life,
> His little, nameless unremembered acts
> Of kindness and of love.[111]

Furthermore, Wordsworth believes that nature can help us enter a meditative state wherein we are imbued, however briefly, with the power of seership:

> Until, the breath of this corporeal frame
> And even the motion of our human blood
> Almost suspended, we are laid asleep
> In body, and become a living soul:
> While with an eye made quiet by the power
> Of harmony, and the deep power of joy,
> We see into the life of things.[112]

Seeing "into the life of things" is not a condition many teenagers have experienced, the "paradise years" of childhood excepted. Yet the *idea* of nature's kinship to the human being resonates profoundly in adolescent souls. Even as some students adamantly refute nature's divine basis publicly, they also seem inwardly reassured that great men and women throughout history have pushed aside some veil to reveal nature's spiritual foundations.

Wordsworth and his fellow poets are constantly searching for ways to reach and prolong this exalted union with nature, which promises to endow them with powers that lift them out of their ordinary consciousness. In "Kubla Khan," Coleridge refers to a mysterious "miracle of rare device,/A sunny pleasure dome with caves of ice" and an "Abyssinian maid" who plays on a dulcimer and sings of Mount Abora. He is certain that

> Could I revive within me
> Her symphony and song,
> To such a deep delight 'twould win me,
> That with music loud and long
> I would build that dome in air,
> That sunny dome! Those caves of ice!
> And all who heard should see them there,
> And all should cry, Beware! Beware!
> His flashing eyes, his floating hair!
> Weave a circle round him thrice,
> And close your eyes with holy dread,
> For he on honey-dew hath fed,
> And drunk the milk of Paradise.[113]

Coleridge tells us he had been in a drug-induced state when the vision described in "Kubla Khan" came to him, a fascination for some students that often seems to overshadow the actual content of the poem. More literary eleventh graders, however, grapple with the surreal tone and possible meaning of the piece. The poet seems to be saying that if he could reawaken his dormant imaginative forces, he could create memorable edifices "in the air"—the element of all singer/poets. Furthermore, he, too, would be able to "lift the veil" of nature's mysteries, an act that somehow fills listeners with "holy dread." Perhaps Coleridge's speaker is like the liberated prisoner in Plato's "Allegory of the Cave," who discovers a higher reality outside the shadows of the cave and then returns to share the truth, only to be met with fear and derision from those still held captive by their comfortable illusions.

One of Coleridge's longer poems, *The Rime of the Ancient Mariner*, takes this idea much further. It is another perfect eleventh grade piece, embodying so many of the year's initiatory themes: the journey, the suffering and isolation, the gradual transformation, the redemption, the return for the purpose of instructing or enriching others. A gaunt and haunted-looking old seaman stops a man hurrying to a wedding and mesmerizes him with the following harrowing tale: On a sea voyage the mariner befriends an albatross that appears as a good omen.

> As if it had been a Christian soul,
> We hailed it in God's name.
> And a good south wind spring up behind:
> The albatross did follow
> And every day, for food or play,
> Came to the mariner's hollo![114]

Then, impelled by some malevolent impulse, the mariner picks up a crossbow and shoots the bird, this envoy of nature, with disastrous results. The winds completely die out for weeks, leaving the ship stalled under a cloudless sky and the men parched.

> And every tongue, through utter drought,
> Was withered at the root;
> We could not speak, no more than if
> We had been choked with soot.[115]

The crew members hang the body of the albatross around the mariner's neck as a grisly reminder of his misdeed. Eerily, and at breakneck speed despite the lack of wind, a skeletal ship approaches upon which two spectral figures throw dice for the sailors' souls. All of his fellow shipmates turn an accusing eye towards the mariner just before they drop dead, leaving him the ship's sole survivor.

Like Gilgamesh before him, the mariner subsequently undergoes a "life-in-death" experience. Surrounded by corpses, and bearing the body of the albatross he himself has killed, the mariner must now do penance. He suffers the ultimate fate of the individual cut off from any human intercourse.

> Alone, alone, all, all alone
> Alone on a wide wide sea!
> And never a saint took pity on
> My soul in agony.[116]

The turning point in his suffering occurs when the mariner finds himself gazing at water-snakes that before had reminded him only of his growing sense of guilt; "a thousand thousand slimy things/Lived on; and so did I."[117] The isolation and the sense of self-loathing are both such familiar conditions to teenagers that the teacher need not draw obvious parallels. It is enough for students to register the mariner's torment; however, they also need to recognize the moment that marks the breaking of the curse.

> I watched their rich attire:
> Blue, glossy green, and velvet black,
> They coiled and swam; and every track
> Was a flash of golden fire.
>
> Oh happy living things! No tongue
> Their beauty might declare:
> A spring of love gushed from my heart,
> And I blessed them unaware...

> That self-same moment I could pray;
> And from my neck so free
> The albatross fell off, and sank
> Like lead into the sea.[118]

Students are quick to note that only when the mariner's attention is drawn *outside himself*, despite his anguish, to the beauty of the creatures curling through the water does it become possible for some inner shift to occur within the mariner.

This presents yet another subtle but crucial lesson for adolescents. We all know that high schoolers tend to focus much of their attention upon themselves. Indeed, it may be the most self-absorbed phase of their entire lives, not surprising when we consider how their blossoming inner realm begins to acquire depth and dimension at this time. However, teenagers must guard against an obsessive self-preoccupation that leads to a general withdrawal from the world. Far too often such isolation can lead to depression, perhaps the fastest-growing diagnosed pathology in the West.

The mariner begins the long road to redemption because he finally looks at the world of nature through the eyes of one who has suffered. His own misery has sown seeds of empathy within him. Like Gilgamesh, Parzival and Prospero before him, the ancient mariner learns the value of compassion, but in his particular case, only after a senseless act of wanton destruction. He has despoiled the natural world, and the supernatural world has answered. The mariner must endure a curse by finding his way to blessing.

Some eleventh graders see Coleridge's poem as the most prophetic of allegories, describing both humanity's accelerating, wanton destruction of the environment and the price we are paying for our contempt. Students will argue that humanity has yet to learn the lesson that the mariner now feels compelled to preach to a stunned but much more sober wedding guest: "He prays the best who loves the best/All creatures great and small." We hark back to Sussman's idea of the initiate returning to the community for its enrichment. Ultimately, it is not enough for the mariner, nor for any of us, to privately repent his violation of nature. He—and we—must now assume a public responsibility, not only for the past, but for the future. It is the type of thought that leads eleventh graders into the large-souled terrain of the senior year.

Twelfth Grade:
Song of Myself, Song of the World

Straddling a Great Threshold

Recently, I hosted an evening attended by parents and middle school students. They had come to hear approximately thirty twelfth graders from four different Waldorf high schools speak about their experiences. The seniors began by recounting their recent, weeklong camping trip to Hermit Island, Maine, where they had studied marine biology by actually wading through the tide pools of the rocky coast. These students did not simply gather specimens; they examined them under microscopes, sketched the creatures and their environments, wrote poems inspired by Rachel Carson's nature writings, painted seascapes, danced and sang together. As they described their activities, a number of twelfth graders expressed appreciation for the hands-on learning opportunities. One girl summed up the whole experience as a reminder that all of nature seemed to be quietly urging, "Pay attention," not only to the spectacular sunsets, but to the understated moments that would otherwise go unnoticed—the skittering of a sand crab across a tide pool floor, the swaying of rockweed in the water, the curving flight of gulls.

Towards the end of the evening, one parent in the audience commented on the students' eloquence, poise and insight. Indeed, these young people exuded an unpretentious self-assurance that seems characteristic of many Waldorf twelfth graders. As contracted and broody as eleventh graders can get, seniors often seem to acquire a new dimension, an expansiveness that was not there before. They stand poised on a great threshold, straddling both the world of the school which they are rapidly outgrowing and the larger world which they generally cannot wait to take by storm. Their vision seems to broaden as their thinking deepens.

To nourish these suddenly "larger souls," we introduce twelfth graders to the literary voices from the past two centuries whose ideas again reflect the concerns these students grapple with daily, especially the question of how to reconcile the tension between the desire to express their ever-strengthening individuality on the one hand and the wish to live in community on the other. In the fall they study excerpts from the great American writers of the nineteenth century—Emerson, Thoreau, Hawthorne, Dickinson, Whitman—with their celebration of an individuality that can encompass the world. Later in the year, the students read works by the great Russian writers—Pushkin, Gogol, Dostoevsky, Tolstoy, Solzhenitsyn—with their passionate yearning for a new brotherhood that can transcend ethnic and national boundaries.

The Birth of American Literature

In the history of the West, we can point to precious few eras where a mysterious concentration of creative forces—like a spiritual magnifying glass—seemed to converge over a small area of the globe, igniting an entire culture. Certainly this occurred in fifth century B.C. Greece, and again in Italy in during the Renaissance. At least in literary terms, the same might be said for nineteenth century New England. Until this period, America's geniuses had marshaled their energies to create a new political system. Culturally, however, this new American nation was considered a primitive backwater. In 1818 a British journalist wrote,

> Americans have no national literature and no learned men. The talents of our transatlantic brethren show themselves chiefly in political pamphlets. The Americans are too young to rival in literature the old nations of Europe. They have neither history, nor romance, nor poetry, nor legends on which to exercise their genius and kindle their imagination. The inhabitants of the United States will never have to boast of a native poetry or a native music.[119]

A year later English critic Sydney Smith echoed this view. "In the four corners of the globe," he inquired, "who reads an American book or goes to an American play or looks at an American painting?"[120] I suspect there were some sour grapes behind this Englishman's opinion, since the Americans had defeated the British in two wars within thirty-five years. Nevertheless, there must have been more than a grain of truth in his estimation of Americans. Aside from Benjamin Franklin's *Autobiography,* Washington Irving's stories and James Fenimore Cooper's *Leatherstocking Tales*, little had emerged from America that it could call its own. None of those authors could be credited with so altering the literary landscape that he inspired a whole generation of new American writers. The nation would have to wait until the 1830s, when an ex-Unitarian minister with piercing blue eyes and a tomahawk nose would proclaim America's "cultural declaration of independence" from Europe.

Ralph Waldo Emerson seemed an unlikely choice to become the father of American letters. Born in 1803 into one of Boston's elite families, he was a sickly child. After following the family tradition of attending Harvard—where he compiled a lackluster record—and becoming a minister, he suffered a crisis of faith when his young wife Ellen died. Emerson left the pulpit, traveled extensively in Europe, met with such literary giants as Thomas Carlyle, Coleridge and Wordsworth, and returned to the States with a renewed sense of purpose. He began to write and lecture, none more influential than his 1836 essay entitled "Nature." In it, he introduced the basic tenets of what was later termed "transcendentalism." When I asked a class of twelfth graders to identify the word inside that word that might offer a clue to its meaning, (thinking of "transcend"), one sly senior volunteered, "Dental?" Another humorist in the class then asked why, at the dentist's office, the Indian mystic refused Novocain; the reason? He wanted to "transcend dental medication!" On some deep level, a literature teacher must fear that students will remember such jokes long after they have forgotten the substance of Emerson's thinking.

In "Nature," Emerson makes three bold assertions: (1) The foundations of Man are not in matter, but in spirit; (2) Man is a god in ruins; and (3) Man is a dwarf of himself. He goes on to say that at one time human beings were glorious, colossal beings in the spiritual sense, but that in time, we have lost many of our spiritual gifts. In our current, diminished state, our spiritual natures now fit us poorly, as oversized garments that completely engulf us remind us of how much we have contracted. For seniors who may have just studied zoology—and particularly Darwin's work—in a course immediately preceding this one, Emerson's assertions challenge the prevailing notions of evolution. He seems to be suggesting a *descent*, rather than an ascent, of humanity.

However far removed we are from our divine origins, Emerson firmly believed in our ability to rekindle our spiritual forces—"the exertions of a power which exists not in time and space, but an instantaneous in-streaming causing power."[121] This ability, says Emerson, which *transcends* the senses and enables us to apprehend higher truths, does not depend upon book knowledge or conventional forms of learning. Indeed, in his electrifying address at Harvard entitled "The American Scholar," he stated categorically,

> The book, the college, the school of art, the institution of any kind, stop with some past utterance of genius. That is good, they say. Let us hold by this. They pin me down. They look backward and not forward. But genius looks forward. Man hopes, genius creates.[122]

I have often asked seniors to imagine sitting among that group of august, older professors and eager young scholars, listening to Emerson challenge his American audience to stop looking for inspiration from Europe.

> We have listened too long to the courtly muses of Europe. The spirit of the American freeman is already suspected to be timid, imitative, tame. ...What is the remedy?...if the single man plant himself indomitably on his instincts and there abide, the huge world will come round to him.[123]

These words resounded as a clarion call to the younger generation in that lecture hall back in 1837. They still do today; twelfth graders certainly understand what Emerson calls the battle between the integrity of the self on the one hand and the demands of society on the other. In "Self-Reliance" he states categorically, "Society everywhere is in conspiracy against the manhood of every one of its members."[124] He places the self on one side of a pitched battle, locked in combat with the forces of a monolithic society arrayed on the other side. At stake is no less a prize than one's own individuality.

Emerson describes the battle in dramatic terms; society uses the lure of conformity to oppose the integrity of one's own mind, the safety of imitation to whittle away the power of originality, the security of the past to suppress the dangerous unpredictability of living in the here and now. What can the individual summon to inoculate himself against the vast, undifferentiated armies of the submissive, with their mindless adoration of what Orwell termed "groupthink"?

Repeatedly Emerson leads his audiences back to the inviolability of the Self. "Nothing is at last sacred but the integrity of your own mind. ...Bid the invaders take the shoes from off their feet, for God is here within."[125] Furthermore, this divinity within invites a present-mindedness, despite the prevailing societal practice of looking back to conventions and traditions of the past for stability's sake. Emerson urges people to live fully in the moment.

> This one fact the world hates; that the self becomes, for that forever degrades the past, turns all riches to poverty, all reputation to a shame, confounds the saint with the rogue, shoves Jesus and Judas equally aside.[126]

Twelfth graders feel keenly this "becoming." Indeed, they are able to look back on their earlier adolescence with an increasing objectivity to see just how much they have matured in a few short years. Seniors have generally passed through that insecure, imitative teenage phase when, in their desire to fit in, they "join the herd"; they wear what their friends wear, parrot "in" slang, rebel against group-approved targets. As they become ever more themselves, seniors begin to value uniqueness wherever they encounter it. The oddballs and eccentrics in the class who used to be considered uncool are now celebrated as quirky—but genuine—individuals. It should not be surprising, then, that Emerson's exhortation to be original appeals so strongly to these young people. When he states, "To believe your own thought, to believe that what is true for you in your private heart is true for all men—that is genius,"[127] he is speaking to their deepest longings for an authentic Self.

One of the key dimensions in the Birth of American Literature is the seniors' exploration of the source of selfhood. We look at all the possible influences that might determine individuality—genetic and environmental; the perennial nature versus nurture argument. After students have made an exhaustive list: gender, physical attributes, age, temperament, talents and interests, family configuration, values, socio-economic status, geographical location, political affiliation, religious beliefs, education, and so forth, I ask them: If we knew all of the above information, would we then be able to pinpoint the Self? We discuss as many examples as possible, particularly cases of people who seem to defy all measures of predictability, who escape the ghetto or the log cabin to become jazz musicians or presidents. We consider twins who grow up under virtually identical circumstances, yet who become wildly divergent individualities. Invariably, we agree that the true Self can never be reduced to labels or classifications or lists—despite the proliferation of internet services that use "twenty-nine measures of compatibility" to match ideal mates. That which makes us truly individual remains a mystery, as elusive as the miraculous moment in each toddler's life when some self-referential light dawns within, enabling us for the first time to utter the word "I."

In the spirit of Emerson's celebration of the self, I have often given twelfth graders another challenge, one of their shortest, and yet most difficult assignments—to write down an "Original Thought," that is, some idea that the students believe has never been expressed before in quite the way the students might formulate it. After publicly complaining that it is an impossible task, that every so-called new thought is just a recast old one, they usually throw themselves into the assignment with relish. A selection of the more thought-provoking results follows.

"Only a still mind can think active thoughts, but don't take my word for it. Try writing a sonnet on a roller coaster."
— Ari Freuman

"Do not jump into a pool without water in it."
— Hiromi Nishizawa

"Too much of a good thing is great!"
— Caitlin Stern

"To reach your dreams, you must wake up."
— Arielle Mendelsohn

"A neat room shows that you have too much spare time."
— Jeb Metric

"Adults don't mature; they just lose their sense of fun."
— Naomi Henderson

"Because people see truths in us that we never realized, we unknowingly become friends to find out more about ourselves."
— Jessica Weinstein

"Friends are like invisible bungee cords that keep us from falling into ourselves."
— Judith Arnold

"A person is often two people. One is who he is with himself; the other is who he is with others. When he can be the same person in both situations, he is his own person."
— Darren Bosch

"Trying to put an original thought into words is like trying to catch water in a net."
— Katie Mueller

Finally, one senior a few years ago—Alec Miller—came up with an original thought that Emerson would have applauded: "Questions are better than answers, because answers are just questions cut short by arrogance." This statement captures the very essence of the Birth of American Literature course. By honoring creative inquiry over conventional answers, it epitomizes the thrust of the entire senior year. We want Waldorf students to think "outside of the box," to approach problems from more than one narrow perspective. Another great American writer, Walt Whitman, referred to this mode of thinking in the beginning of "Song of Myself."

> You shall no longer take things at second or third hand,
> Nor look through the eyes of the dead, nor feed on the spectres in books;
> You shall not look through my eyes either, nor take things from me,
> You shall listen to all sides and filter them from yourself.[128]

In this listening "to all sides" and filtering "them from yourself," Whitman describes what I have heard wise Waldorf high school teachers term "aspect thinking." It really takes the notion of empathy discussed earlier in *Gilgamesh* and *Parzival* and *The Tempest* one step further.

What does it take to empathize with another person? We need an imaginative leap to see and feel some situation through the eyes of another. Aspect thinking is an extension of the idea of empathy, but on a cognitive level. It means thinking through an idea or situation from a number of different vantage points. Can young people develop mobility in their thinking so that they can argue an issue from a number of points of view? We all know "The Blind Men and the Elephant" illustration. Aspect thinking involves a similar dynamic, but goes even a step beyond that, because the blind men were each limited by their own experiences; one thought the tail was a rope, another thought the side a wall, another thought the leg a tree trunk. Our hope is that twelfth graders can begin to not only see an idea from different perspectives but synthesize those perspectives as well in some meaningful way.

Studying Emerson, Thoreau, Hawthorne, Whitman and Dickinson gives twelfth graders the perfect opportunity to exercise this capacity of aspect thinking. Each of these authors provides a unique viewpoint of human nature. Reading excerpts from *Walden*, seniors see how Thoreau turns Emerson's philosophizing about self-reliance into an uncompromising code of conduct. Many students who struggle to follow Emerson's more conceptual musings find firmer footing in Thoreau's world. Some appreciate his earthier, anecdotal style, his ability to "put legs under Emerson's ideas." In the process, Thoreau appears the more will-oriented and practical of the two men. His exhortation to "simplify, simplify" strikes a chord in some young people who see the proliferation of electronic gadgetry in their own lives and who cannot remember the last time they spent more than eight waking hours without the company of a cell phone, iPod, television, or computer.

Most of these seniors encounter Thoreau's ideas just as their own lives become increasingly clogged by the complexities of the college selection process. A number of them recognize a kindred spirit in his rejection of others' expectations, of delayed gratification, of the pursuit of society's version of success. "Rather than love, than money, than fame, give me truth."[129] Like Emerson, he reinforces in them an awareness of their own power to consciously shape not only the arc of their future, but even this very day.

> It is something to be able to paint a particular picture, or to carve a statue, and so make a few objects beautiful; but it is far more glorious to carve and paint the very atmosphere and medium through which we look, which morally we can do. To affect the quality of the day, that is the highest of arts.[130]

Of course Thoreau takes this idea much further in his famous stance on civil disobedience. Again, for young people striving to achieve a measure of independence, his words fortify and embolden when he writes:

> This American government—what is it but a tradition…each instant losing some of its integrity. It has not the vitality and force of a single living man. If the law is of such a nature that it requires you to be an agent of injustice to another, then, I say, break the law. . . .

> I was not born to be forced. I will breathe after my own fashion. Let us see who is strongest. What force has a multitude? They only can force me who obey a higher law than I.[131]

Students are impressed to discover that Thoreau's "On the Duty of Civil Disobedience" was one of the greatest influences on the twentieth century's two most highly regarded civil rights leaders—Mohandas Gandhi and Martin Luther King, Jr. Both attributed to Thoreau's essay much of their formative thinking about nonviolent resistance to repressive laws.

Twelfth graders also delight in the oft-told story of Thoreau's protest against the Mexican War, when he refused to pay his poll tax. Although he spent only one night in the Concord jail, Thoreau allegedly received a visit from a hastily dressed Emerson. From outside the jail, Emerson reputedly shouted, "Henry David, what are you doing in there?" Whereupon, Thoreau replied, "Ralph Waldo, what are you doing out there?" Adhering to the dictates of his conscience makes Thoreau a worthy role model in the eyes of some idealistic high school students.

Yet other seniors find Thoreau's voice shrill and judgmental. Emerson may be cerebral, his line of reasoning digressive and elusive at times, but ultimately he wishes only to empower his audience, to have them trust in the immensity of their own souls and the genius of their own minds. Thoreau is more pointed in his critique of people enslaved by their own pursuit of possessions.

> I see young men, my townsmen, whose misfortune it is to have inherited farms, houses, barns, cattle and farming tools; for these are more easily acquired than got rid of. ...Who made them serfs of the soil?...
> Most of the luxuries, and many of the so-called comforts of life, are not only indispensable, but positive hindrances to the elevation of mankind.[132]

Despite his assertion that "I desire that there may be as many different persons in the world as possible; but I would have each one be very careful to find out and pursue his own way,"[133] Thoreau is not shy about suggesting how people should live.

> Cultivate poverty like a garden herb, like sage. Do not trouble yourself much to get new things, whether clothes or friends. Turn the old; return to them. Things do not change; we change. Sell your clothes and keep your thoughts.[134]

After reading such prescriptive remedies for his misguided neighbors, some students see Thoreau as little more than a finger-wagging scold, upbraiding people for committing themselves to long-term responsibilities, for being charitable, or for preferring comforts over deprivations. These students see hypocrisy everywhere in Thoreau's life; they point to the gap between the impression he gives his readers about living in the Walden "wilderness" and the actuality. Thoreau's cabin was only a mile from the center of Concord. He had easy access to human commerce and to his mother's house; she often cooked for him and did his laundry. According to these detractors, Thoreau was hardly the self-reliant, solitary poet he made himself out to be.

Another aspect of Walden has troubled many students. In "Higher Laws," Thoreau makes a bewildering statement. After venerating nature throughout his writing, he suddenly declares, "Nature is hard to be overcome, but she must be overcome."[135] In the context of the entire chapter, students see that he is referring to a lower nature found in the human being. "We are conscious of an animal in us, which awakens in proportion as our higher nature slumbers."[136] To this lower nature, Thoreau attributes all "impure" acts, all forms of sensuality, and it is this sensuality that must be suppressed. Interestingly, the man who accused his neighbors of superfluous labor links the control of sensuality to work. "From exertion come wisdom and purity; from sloth ignorance and sensuality."[137] Needless to say, young people for whom sensuality is a natural expression of their burgeoning affections find Thoreau's stance rather prudish.

This puritanical strain also emerges strongly in Nathaniel Hawthorne's work. Although he was a neighbor of Emerson and Thoreau in Concord in the 1840s, he could hardly be considered one of their transcendental circle. Indeed, Hawthorne's short stories provide a vivid contrast to the elevated estimation of human beings' possibilities that Emerson and Thoreau affirm. Hawthorne's writings stem from a darker side of America's heritage, when mesmerizing voices such as the seventeenth century Puritan minister Jonathan Edwards would shake his congregation's souls in apocalyptic sermons such as "Sinners in the Hands of an Angry God."

> The God that holds you over the pit of hell, much as one holds a spider, or some loathsome insect over the fire, abhors you, and is dreadfully provoked: his wrath towards you burns like fire; he looks upon you as worthy of nothing else, but to be cast into the fire; he is of purer eyes than to bear to have you in his sight; you are ten thousand times more abominable in his eyes, than the most hateful venomous serpent is in ours. You have offended him infinitely more than ever a stubborn rebel did his prince; and yet it is nothing but his hand that holds you from falling into the fire every moment.[138]

It is this depiction of the guilt-ridden human heart—so susceptible to evil forces and perched on the verge of eternal damnation—that Hawthorne probes in his writing. Interestingly, he traces his own family roots back to the Puritan period; his great grandfather, Judge Hathorne, presided over the Salem witch trials.

Students can clearly see this puritanical influence in such stories as "Young Goodman Brown." A young man leaves his wife, heavy-handedly named Faith, in the middle of the night and heads into the forbidding forest to keep an appointment with a mysterious figure who turns out to be the Devil. Goodman Brown then finds himself and a veiled young woman, who appears to be Faith, as central participants in some satanic rite. During the ceremony, he is shocked to see the town's most seemingly upright citizens mingling familiarly with scoundrels and sinners. Worse, Goodman Brown himself feels "a loathful brotherhood by sympathy of all that was wicked in his heart." Only when the presiding Devil declares, "Ye had still hoped that virtue were all a dream. Now ye are undeceived ...Evil is the nature of mankind!"[139] does Goodman Brown try to stop the proceedings. "Look up to heaven and resist the wicked one!"[140]

Goodman Brown awakens the next morning in the deserted forest, uncertain whether the experiences of the previous night actually happened or were a nightmarish dream. In one crucial regard it does not matter, because Goodman Brown returns to town shaken and transformed, now full of doubts about his wife's and the town folk's virtue. Although he speaks to no one of his foray into the woods, his deepening suspicions cast a daily pall over all of his interactions. He grows distant from his Faith and eyes his neighbors with mistrust. He lives the remainder of his life as a self-created loner, imprisoned and embittered by his own disillusionment.

Hawthorne gives his readers a twisted, shadow image of Thoreau's aforementioned idea about the individual's ability "to affect the quality of the day; that is the highest of the arts." Goodman Brown has, indeed, altered the quality of his days; his festering doubts have poisoned his life and spawned his own living hell. Such a story is another potent illustration for seniors of the power they possess, positive and negative, to alter their daily landscape by adjusting their own attitude to life's vicissitudes.

Many twelfth graders admire Hawthorne's craft as a writer and understand his preoccupation with the darker regions of the soul, for they are also drawn to the crosscurrents that afflict the human heart. However, as with Dante's worldview, few of today's students can relate to this puritanical idea of original sin spreading like a great stain over a person's life. Rather, they find in Whitman's exuberant celebration of humanity an expression of their own expanding, seemingly limitless, selves.

Whitman's work is a revelation to most twelfth graders, even to those who have some familiarity with contemporary poetry. As soon as they read the first lines of "Song of Myself," they realize that they are witnessing a literary revolution:

> I celebrate myself, and sing myself,
> And what I assume you shall assume,
> For every atom belonging to me as good belongs to you.
>
> I loafe and invite my soul,
> I lean and loafe at my ease observing a spear of
> summer grass.
>
> My tongue, every atom of my blood, form'd from this
>   soil, this air,
> Born here of parents born here from parents the same,
>   and their parents the same,
> I, now thirty-seven years old in perfect health begin,
> Hoping to cease not till death.[141]

Before Whitman, no poet had ever freed himself so entirely from conventional forms to create a verse unfettered by predictable meters. The blank verse that arose in the sixteenth century liberated poets from the strictures of rhyme, but it still proceeded according to a more or less measured iambic pentameter. Three hundred years later, even in writing about their groundbreaking subject matter, Wordsworth and Coleridge did not venture outside the bounds of blank verse.

Whitman shatters the mold; students see immediately why he is revered as "the father of modern poetry." He writes in a voice never before expressed on paper, in long, unrestrained lines that rely almost exclusively on rising and falling cadences to convey their music. Beyond his stylistic pioneering, Whitman is the American poet Emerson had sought in his essay "The Poet," who could "chaunt our own times and social circumstance," who, like Dante, would dare to write his autobiography into universality.

Of all the writers that seniors read during their high school careers, Whitman's may be the voice closest to those twelfth graders' own. His "Song of Myself" is like an anthem for young people who are questioning every convention and creed they have ever encountered. When he writes, "Logic and sermons never convince, the damp of the night drives deeper into my soul,"[142] he is speaking for every adolescent who has felt bored or betrayed by the sterility and remoteness of "textbook teaching." Whitman exults in the lessons of direct, unadulterated experience; after reading his poetry, seniors feeling stifled by the sheltering cocoons of school and home can hardly contain their impulse to "escape" into the wider world. Just as Whitman embraces all—the "kept woman, sponger, thief, are invited/the heavy-lipped slave is invited, the venerealee is invited"[143]—so these young adults want to burst through the walls of their circumscribed lives and to mingle with a new universe of people.

Part of Whitman's appeal to these twelfth graders is the expansiveness of his vision. Just as they feel life's possibilities rising within them, he describes the grand scale and cosmic design behind every individual's existence.

> Immense have been the preparations for me,
> Faithful and friendly the arms that have help'd me.
> Cycles ferried my cradle, rowing and rowing like cheerful boatmen,
> For room to me stars kept aside in their own rings,
> They sent influences to look after what was to hold me.[144]

On the one hand, Whitman's writing teems with spiritual insight, an "Emersonian" sense that the material world is an emblem of divine workings. On the other, he is the most frankly sensual of poets, a stark contrast to Thoreau's puritanical streak. If Emerson is primarily concerned with the life of the mind, and Thoreau with the will, i.e., the practical application of those ideas, then Whitman is surely the poet of feeling.

> I believe in the flesh and the appetites,
> Seeing, hearing, feeling, are miracles, and each
>   part and tag of me is a miracle.
> Divine am I inside and out, and I make holy
>   whatever I touch or am touch'd from,
> The scent of these arm-pits aroma finer than
>   prayer...[145]

Part of Whitman's genius derives from his "tearing of the veil" between the bodily and the spiritual. He reveres them equally; they interpenetrate and suffuse one another. For young people seeking both earthly pleasures and deeper truths, Whitman offers the best of both worlds by melding them into a single pursuit.

Perhaps most reassuring of all, he reinforces Emerson's and Thoreau's emphasis on the primacy of the self.

> I have said that the soul is not greater than the body,
> And that the body is not more than the soul,
> And nothing, not God, is more to one than one's
>   self is.[146]

To the devoutly religious or the self-effacing, Whitman may sound like an egomaniac, but to many seniors looking for affirmation in their quest for an authentic, large-souled self, his words serve as an inspiration.

One of the seniors' favorite challenges in this course is to write their own "Song of Myself." We encourage them to celebrate their strengths, to describe themselves from different angles, to trumpet their surprising and varied dimensions. Here are two excerpts:

> I am not always positive and vital,
> You will find me a stagnant glass of grape juice growing
>   mold upon the desk,
> I am the queen of spades,
> I require the company of procrastinators, and cynics;
> They are part of me, I become them.
> I am the critic as well as the artist, and parts of me are
> Morbid and morose.
> I am envy;
> It is my favorite of the seven sins.
> I cannot look away from the poor boy who, thinking himself
>   worthless, takes the eternal pills.
> I am filled with tragedy, cynicism is my feeble wooden
>   shield.
> I lace my soul with pain, and drought,
> And the blood-colored wine overflows the chalice.
> – Julian Russo '02

> I am an underestimated question
> Like, "pickles and onions with that?" or "do you have this
>   color in a size four?"
> I am best described without music—I am soundless—
>   like the non-sound of alarm clocks that make you
>   late for school, or the nonexistent "ding" of burnt
>   cookies.
> I doubt the certain, and am certain of the doubtful.
> I'm convinced vitamin C is a hoax
>   while I believe in fairies and ghosts...
> – Kate Rudish '06

Whether their focus is on their shadow sides or their higher selves, whether their voices are somber or whimsical, these seniors usually appreciate the opportunity to write unapologetically about themselves. It is as if reading Whitman gives young people permission, first to uncover, then to share the inner treasures they have secretly been laying up over the course of their childhood and adolescence.

Parents and teachers, too, have much to learn from Whitman. I have been asked by desperate parents what is the appropriate stance to take with their often rude or rebellious teenagers. The commanding "Because I said so!" no longer works, nor does the sheltering "mother hen" gesture of earlier childhood. Whitman favors a different posture:

> Each (young) man and each (young) woman of you I lead upon a knoll,
> My left hand hooking you round the waist,
> My right hand pointing to landscapes of continents and the public road.
> Not I, not anyone else can travel that road for you,
> You must travel it for yourself.[147]

With older adolescents, we can no longer be the authorities who compel obedience; however, we would be equally mistaken to assume that they are now full-fledged adults, and thereby abdicate our roles as parents and teachers. Whitman describes an approach that both supports and empowers these young people. He acknowledges that our rightful relationship with older teenagers cannot involve pushing from below nor yanking from above; rather, we need to stand shoulder-to-shoulder and point to life's possibilities. Young people don't need gurus or tyrants; they need guides who understand that their role is to gradually make themselves obsolete.

If Whitman doubles as the convivial companion and muse who escorts young people for a brief but rousing ramble along their life path, Emily Dickinson is the solitary soul who ventures no further than her garden gate. Her biography, as well as her poetic voice, strikes most twelfth graders as diametrically opposed to Whitman's. Where he traveled widely, lived in the teeming environs of Brooklyn and became editor of one of its daily newspapers, Emily Dickinson lived a circumscribed life in Amherst, Massachusetts, rarely leaving the family home during the last twenty years of her life. Her self-effacing nature was legendary; she left instructions to have her more than eighteen hundred poems burned after her death, a request with which her sister Lavinia fortunately did not comply. In describing herself in a letter, Dickinson wrote, "I am small, like the wren, and my hair is bold like the chestnut burr, and my eyes like the sherry in the glass that the guest leaves."[148]

While Whitman's poetry is sprawling, effusive, frankly revealing, Dickinson's voice is spare, elliptical, enigmatic. Whitman is considered the poet of the panoramic and overflowing, Dickinson of the confined and reserved. Yet discerning twelfth graders over the years have credited her poetry with containing the same immensities as Whitman's. Appreciating Dickinson's work is no easy task. She demands much of her readers; many students see no further than her constrained, rhyming quatrains that, at first glance, appear to exude all the sentiment of a Hallmark card. Yet beneath the surface of her lines, true poetry connoisseurs can discover miniature universes vaster than their imaginations can fully comprehend. Dickinson is full of paradoxes, as inwardly bold as she is outwardly diffident.

This disparity between the appearance and actuality, between seeming simplicity and layers of complexity, both in her life and in her work, emerges as a central subject in her poetry.

> The outer from the inner
> Derives its magnitude—
> 'Tis duke, or dwarf, according
> As is the central mood—

> The fine unvarying axis
> That regulates the wheel,
> Though spokes spin more conspicuous
> And fling a dust the while
>
> The inner paints the outer;
> The brush without the hand
> Its picture publishes, precise
> As is the inner brand
>
> On fine arterial canvas—
> A cheek, perchance a brow
> The stars' whole secret in the lake
> Eyes were not meant to know.[149]

The poem itself embodies Dickinson's theme. The "outer" experience of the piece—precise, regulated, unvarying trimeter—can lull students at first into a cursory, sing-song reading. The "secret" remains undetected until they probe beneath the surface "of the lake," less with their eyes than with their minds. Thinking along the same thought paths as Emily Dickinson is one of the most formidable challenges any twelfth grader will every face. Her poems often pose riddles; they are like rooms that must be unlocked before they can be entered and the furnishings fully admired. Entry is never assured. Dickinson is exceedingly discriminating about her visitors.

> The soul selects her own society
> Then shuts the door
> On her divine majority
> Obtrude no more
>
> Unmoved, she notes the chariot's pausing
> At her low gate
> Unmoved, the emperor is kneeling
> Upon her mat

> I've known her from an ample nation
> Choose one;
> Then close the valves of her attention
> Like stone.[150]

When we study this piece, I ask students which word is the most potent in the poem. Most of them settle on "valves," for its brilliant double meaning. Of course, the heart has valves, but so do cold, soulless machines, and the overtones of both associations resonate throughout the poem. Coupled with the abruptness of the final line that feels like a slamming door, Dickinson's design once again reinforces the content.

Seniors who are drawn to Dickinson's work appreciate her economy and her craftsmanship, but they also marvel at the surprises that surface in her poems. Some find it shocking that it is Dickinson who writes, "If I feel physically as if the top of my head were taken off, I know that is poetry."[151] Her own work has that explosive quality, like quiet detonations in small chambers. Reading one of her poems is like holding a hand grenade disguised as a pineapple; it looks harmless enough until the readers find and then pull the pin.

> No rack can torture me,
> My soul's at liberty,
> Behind this mortal bone
> There knits a bolder one
>
> You cannot prick with saw
> Nor rend with scimitar.
> Two bodies therefore be
> Bind one, and one will flee
>
> The eagle of his nest
> No easier divest
> And gain the sky,
> Than mayest thou,

> Except thyself may be
> Thine enemy;
> Captivity's consciousness,
> So's liberty.[152]

One of the great lessons Dickinson offers young people has to do with freedom, and from whence it arises. Most teenagers identify freedom with mobility; the keys to the car are the symbol of this linkage. Sitting behind the wheel and driving somewhere—anywhere—is every adolescent's dream. It gives instant credibility to their belief that they are now "grown up," no longer so dependent upon parents and other adults. Yet Dickinson challenges this view that freedom is expressed only outwardly. One twelfth grader once remarked that the idea embodied in those four loaded words—"Captivity's consciousness,/So's liberty"—was a recasting of a familiar idea that she had come across before but could not quite recall where or when. Aided by a little class investigation, she traced the concept back to Hamlet's famous line, "There's nothing good or bad but thinking makes it so."[153] Indeed, both Shakespeare and Dickinson anticipate the modern dilemma—that external constraints no longer threaten our freedoms as much as internal impediments do, what William Blake referred to as "mind-forged manacles."[154]

Usually, after the twelfth graders complete the Birth of American Literature course, teachers can sense a marked change in the students. They still complain, of course, about the pressure of the college application process, and about their homework load, and about the "childish" school rules they must follow. However, many seniors now seem less apologetic about their personal quirks and foibles; they appear more intellectually inquisitive, more inwardly comfortable living within their own paradoxes than before they met the ideas of Emerson, Thoreau, Hawthorne, Whitman and Dickinson. They seem readier than ever to accept the notion that they are the authors of their own lives.

Goethe's *Faust*: Encounter with Evil

A telling sign that young people are maturing is the degree to which they assume responsibility for their actions. That is why introducing them to Goethe's *Faust* around the same time as they read the writers in the American literature course can put this idea of the authorship of one's life into the sharpest possible perspective. At its core, *Faust* is a play about human accountability. The story line is well known, even archetypal. A brilliant scholar becomes so disenchanted with life, so disillusioned by his own inability to attain spiritual illumination that his thoughts turn to suicide. He is momentarily saved by the grace of an angelic choir singing Easter hymns. However, in his vulnerable state, Faust is visited by the devil, disguised first as a dog, then as a wandering scholar, appareled much like Faust himself.

Usually, at least one astute senior will recall that the devil encountered by Young Goodman Brown in Hawthorne's short story bears a striking likeness to the protagonist.

> As nearly as could be discerned, the second
> traveller was about fifty years old, apparently
> in the same rank of life as Goodman Brown,
> and bearing a considerable resemblance
> to him, though perhaps more in expression
> than features. Still, they might have been
> taken for father and son.[155]

What is the meaning of these resemblances between the human and the devilish? Goethe's Mephisto alludes to one possible answer when he says, "Gone is the Nordic phantom that former ages saw;/You see no horns, no tail or claw.../The Evil One is gone, the evil ones remain. ..."[156] The implication is that the devil now dons a familiar human guise—the better to blend in with his "target group." If this is true, people would ensure the devil's success either by misguidedly looking in some remote, supernatural realm for a diabolical figure who commits random acts of evil from afar, or by denying his existence altogether. As the adage goes, "The devil's best trick is to persuade us he doesn't exist at all."

In Goethe's version, Faust strikes a deal with the devil; Mephisto will be Faust's "servant" in this life, vice versa in the next. Faust is so cavalier about the afterlife that he agrees almost immediately.

> Of the beyond I have no thought...
> My joys come from this earth, and there,
> That sun has burnt on my despair:
> Once I have left those, I don't care...[157]

> I loathe the knowledge I once sought
> In sensuality's abysmal land
> Let our passions drink their fill.[158]

So the devil ensnares Faust; together they set off on a whirlwind tour of life's pleasures, "the most painful excess." Once he has signed over his immortal soul, Faust is entirely in Mephisto's power. With his "servant's" considerable influence, Faust falls obsessively in love with a young girl, Gretchen. Yet this love is quickly tainted; in short order Faust unwittingly gives Gretchen's mother a fatal sleeping potion, seduces the girl, kills her brother in a swordfight, and then flees with Mephisto before learning that Gretchen is pregnant. While Faust is away, diverted by revels in the presence of Mephisto, witches, and all manner of other evildoers, Gretchen is imprisoned and sentenced to death for drowning her infant child.

One simply cannot read the events that transpire in *Faust* without considering the arc of evil in the world today. Twelfth graders actually relish this exploration of evil. Having met various shadow sides of themselves earlier in their high school careers, they seem eager to confront the underbelly of the world, as simultaneously repellent and alluring as it can be. In no other piece of literature before *Faust* do they meet evil so unapologetically revealed, or a devil who so delights in the disasters he orchestrates. What's compelling about the story, however, is not Mephisto's fiendishness but Faust's flawed humanity. He is caught, as we all are, between higher and lower impulses cohabiting within our souls. When Faust agonizingly confesses:

> Two souls, alas, are dwelling in my breast,
> And one is striving to forsake its brother.
> Unto the world in grossly loving zest,
> With clinging tendrils, one adheres:
> The other rises forcibly in quest
> Of rarefied ancestral spheres.[159]

he is stating a fundamental truth about the human condition. This is familiar territory to Waldorf twelfth graders. As far back as tenth grade, they read a portion of the *Bhagavad-Gita* that speaks of the eternal Atman, or spark of the divine in every human being, which discards the physical body in the same manner that we take off a garment. That same year, they read in the New Testament Jesus' admonition to "render unto Caesar the things which are Caesar's, and unto God the things that are God's,"[160] another acknowledgement of our spiritual/material nature. Hamlet prefigures Faust's ambivalence when he describes the paradox of being human:

> What a piece of work is man! How noble
> in reason! how infinite in faculties! in form and
> moving, how express and admirable! in action how
> like an angel! in apprehension, how like a god! the
> beauty of the world! the paragon of animals! And
> yet, to me, what is this quintessence of dust?[161]

The aforementioned American writers turn this duality into a primary theme, none more explicitly than Dickinson.

> Death is a dialogue between
> The spirit and the dust.
> "Dissolve," says Death. The Spirit, "Sir,
> I have another trust."
>
> Death doubts it, argues from the ground.
> The Spirit turns away,
> Just laying off, for evidence,
> An overcoat of clay.[162]

So the idea of individuals being torn between their spiritual and material inheritances is hardly unique. However, because of people's susceptibility to evil, Goethe's *Faust* provokes some hard questions about the nature of human accountability. When Faust finally discovers the enormity of the chain of events ignited by his initial infatuation, he rails at Mephisto.

> *Faust:* Dog! Abominable monster!...Save her [Gretchen] or woe unto you! The
> most hideous curse upon you for millenniums!
> *Mephisto:* Save her! Who was it that plunged her into ruin? I or you?[163]

The whole of the play hinges upon Mephisto's questions. Is Faust responsible for the catastrophic consequences of his actions? Is Gretchen? Is anyone who commits some wickedness and then proclaims, "The devil made me do it"?

The subject of evil is fascinating for seniors to discuss but, not surprisingly, nearly impossible to reach much agreement about. Some students reject the whole notion of evil, calling it an outmoded construct of religious zealots. Such students endorse what might be described as a kind of "moral relativism"; what one culture might find abhorrent—say, human sacrifice—another culture legalizes under the euphemistic phrase "capital punishment." Other twelfth graders—and even some American political leaders—believe that good and evil are absolutes and absolutely clear to anyone who shares their values. Still others, less certain of their moral compass, grapple with fundamental questions:

- Is evil extrinsic or intrinsic to human nature?
- Is evil necessary?
- Are we free to choose evil?
- Are there degrees of evil?

To aid them in their explorations, I ask students to read a *New York Times Magazine* article written in the mid1990s by Ron Rosenbaum entitled "Staring into the Heart of the Heart of Darkness." While it was written before the world-changing events of September 11, 2001, the article refers to other incidents that raise the specter of evil: the Oklahoma City bombing, the drowning of Susan Smith's children, Jeffrey Dahmer's grisly serial murders, the Menendez brothers' slaying of their parents. In each case, Rosenbaum comes back to the question that gnaws at most of us whenever we are confronted with the inescapability of wickedness in the world: "Why, if there is a God, does He permit an evil like child murder to take place without intervening?"[164]

This inquiry into metaphysics usually leads twelfth graders into a consideration of free will. In *Faust*, the devil lobbies God to be allowed access to Faust, insisting that if God is in a betting mood, "You'll lose him yet to me..."

> The Lord replies,
> "As long as he may be alive,
> So long you shall not be prevented.
> Man errs as long as he shall strive."[165]

The implications here are enormous: (1) that the devil is one of God's underlings and actually must ask for a kind of "authorization" to try to corrupt human beings; (2) that God is in control of affairs on earth, and therefore permits the existence of evil in the world;

(3) that human beings have the ability to "strive," in other words, they possess the free will to resist evil and choose the good. Many seniors challenge Goethe's first two assumptions about the existence of some divine or diabolical figures gambling for human souls. However, young people nearly always endorse the idea of free will. As one twelfth grader wrote in a superb paper on the nature of evil:

> The truth is, it's easier to change the world than to change human nature, because we cannot directly change other people. They will always have the freedom to follow whichever path they choose, be it good, bad, or in between. But we do have the power to change ourselves, if only to become a bit more aware of the consequences of our actions. We have to remember that we are free, and we must take responsibility to use this freedom towards creating the good.
> — Lily Chapin '97

Reading such words can be heartening. Despite the current state of the world, plagued by what could be termed the widespread effects of evil—acts of terrorism, persistent violence, rampant hunger and suffering—many high school students remain optimistic about their capacity to solve such problems. If they have been exposed to the wellsprings of great literature, young people will not readily succumb to cynicism or despair. It is in the nature of adolescents to envision life's possibilities far more than its limitations, to be buoyed and guided rather than to be deflated by the ideals swelling within them. Reading *Faust* usually awakens twelfth graders to both the dark forces that inhabit human souls and the personal power they possess to counteract those forces. It reminds them that the choices they make can have huge implications, not only for themselves but for the countless circles of people expanding outward from every individual center point.

Russian Literature: Regaining the Spirit through Suffering

For young people steeped in the individualistic tradition of classical Western literature, it is always a revelation to be introduced to Russian writers. From Homer's *The Odyssey* to Toni Morrison's *Beloved*, Western writers have focused on the journey of, or threats to the integrity of, the Self. Twelfth graders have on occasion remarked that, when reading Russian literature, they feel as if they encounter something more than the individual author, something more akin to the folk soul of the Russian people. Dostoevsky himself would have certainly agreed; when he was traveling in Europe, he wrote that he felt "like a slice cut away from the loaf." The Russian people have always seemed to possess closer ties than their Western counterparts to their land, to their language and to their fellow countrymen. This may be due, in no small measure, to being a closed society for centuries. When the Mongolian Tatars invaded Russia in the thirteenth century, a shroud of Eastern mysticism fell over the land. Ivan the Terrible liberated Russia from Tatar rule at the end of the fifteenth century. However, instead of permitting the development of individual freedoms, Ivan's reign only paved the way for generations of continued tsarist repression and further isolation from the rest of the world. By the time Peter the Great finally began to open Russia up to influences from the West in the eighteenth century, Russia had slumbered through the intellectual ferment of the high Middle Ages, the Renaissance, and the Reformation.

The image of the sleeping giant certainly seems to capture much of Russia's pre-Revolution history. In stories around the world, we also come across this motif; often it represents a vital loss of consciousness. In the ancient epic of *Gilgamesh*, the central character sleeps for seven days after crossing the Sea of Death and entering a spiritual realm. He wants to acquire the secret of eternal life from the Utnapishtim, but simply being in the presence of divine beings overpowers him. Later, when he has in his possession the flower that will give him "new life," Gilgamesh once again falls asleep, during which a serpent devours his last hope. At critical junctures in *The Odyssey*, when the usually alert and sharp-witted Odysseus falls asleep, his crew becomes mutinous, and calamity ensues. First they open Odysseus' gift from Aeolus, a bag containing the world's untamed winds; their impulsive action raises the tempest that delays Odysseus' return to Ithaka for a decade. Later, as Odysseus lies sleeping, his starving crew decide to ignore his admonition not to eat the sacred herds of Apollo, resulting in yet another storm, this one fatal for many of Odysseus' men. In Shakespeare's *The Tempest*, Prospero reveals the secret of their exile to his young, innocent daughter, then casts a slumber upon her as he executes his plan for revenge.

In the first two examples above, falling asleep has disastrous consequences. It often does when sleep overcomes us in situations such as driving a car that require wakefulness. However, in *The Tempest*, sleep serves other functions; it seems to soften the harshness of the truths Miranda has just learned, and it shields her from knowledge of the unpleasant events Prospero has already set in motion.

Russia's slumber through the centuries possesses aspects of both of these effects. Prevented from enjoying the personal liberties and cultural riches that characterized the West since the Middle Ages, Russia was also shielded—until the last century—from the worst excesses of both rationalism and materialism. Instead, the Russian people developed a strong, even devotional feeling for spiritual life. Until the Bolshevik Revolution rudely awakened the sleeping giant by plunging the Russian population into a forced acceptance of Western industrialization, the people themselves retained a type of innocence, a "Miranda consciousness."

We can experience this almost childlike quality of the Russian folk soul most clearly in their fairy tales. I ask the seniors to read two classic fairy tales at the very beginning of the course in Russian Literature: "Vasilisa and Baba Yaga" and "The Firebird." As with many such tales, both stories begin with loss: death has taken Vasilisa's mother, while in "The Firebird" some thief is stealing

King Berenday's golden apples. Vasilisa suffers the misfortune of being mistreated by her stepmother and two stepsisters while her father is away. As the youngest, she must perform all manner of unreasonable tasks, including the dangerous mission of journeying to the horrible hut of the crone Baba Yaga to fetch some light.

Ivan is also the youngest of three brothers. His two elder brothers fail to catch the thief because they *fall asleep* while keeping watch under the golden apple tree, but Ivan stays awake long enough to see the firebird pluck an apple. The king then commands his three sons to go off in search of the firebird. Early in his journey, Ivan loses his horse to a hungry wolf, but the wolf then reappears to offer aid in Ivan's quest.

Vasilisa also has a "helper," a doll that her mother gave her before she died. The doll completes many of Vasilisa's most oppressive chores while Vasilisa *sleeps*.

Baba Yaga is a fearsome figure, who lives in a cottage made of human bones and skulls and who devours children. Vasilisa narrowly escapes only when the old hag *falls asleep*. The resourceful girl takes with her a skull that serves her well when she returns home. A laser-like light glows from the eyes of the skull, mesmerizing the sisters and stepmother. They cannot look away; slowly the light begins to scorch them, until nothing is left but cinders. Where Vasilisa buries the skull in the garden, a beautiful rosebush sprouts. Her father returns, and father and daughter live happily thereafter.

Ivan's search for the firebird leads him to the palaces of three kings. In the first kingdom, the wolf warns Ivan to take the firebird but to not touch its golden cage. However, Ivan cannot resist the allure of the glittering golden cage; as soon as he grabs it, the king's guards seize Ivan and bring him to the king. Ivan's "sentence" is to journey to a second kingdom, where he must capture and bring back a horse with a golden mane. The wolf once again agrees to help Ivan, but cautions him to not take the horse's golden bridle. The mission goes well until Ivan sees the shining bridle and is unable to keep his hands off it. Again, he is arrested and required to bring back a third king's golden-haired daughter to the second king.

Ivan's remorse convinces the wolf to act on Ivan's behalf. Relying on his ability to alter his appearance at will, the wolf is able to outwit the three kings and secure all three golden treasures—the princess, the horse and the firebird—for the acquisitive Ivan.

At this point in the tale, twelfth graders begin to howl with indignation at the turn of events. What has Ivan done to earn these rewards, they demand. He's the most undeserving "hero" in all of fairytale-dom! All he has shown is a deplorable lack of impulse control, like a spoiled child who sneaks cookies out of the forbidden jar and then, just for expressing his regret, receives a slice of cake as well.

However, because karmic justice usually prevails in fairy tales, I remind the students that the story is not over. On his return journey, Ivan is discovered by his two empty-handed brothers. Driven by envy over his ill-gotten gains, the brothers slay Ivan and return to their father's kingdom, claiming Ivan's spoils as their own and coercing the princess into silence. For ninety days Ivan's body lies unattended, until the wolf once again happens upon him. After obtaining the waters of life, the wolf restores Ivan.

> Prince Ivan sat up rubbing his eyes.
> "How soundly I have slept," he exclaimed.
> "But for me you would have slept forever," replied the grey wolf.[166]

Having gone through death and "resurrection," Ivan returns to his kingdom just in time to prevent the princess' marriage to one of the brothers. Upon seeing her beloved, the princess reveals the brothers' wickedness, and the king dispatches them to the deepest dungeon in the realm. Ivan and his princess then wed and live in harmony thereafter.

For Waldorf seniors, reading such fairy tales is both an intellectual challenge and a sentimental journey. Many of them remember fondly that fairy tales comprised the basis of most of their education in first grade; their introduction to letters, numbers, and drawing all flowed out of these stories. Now, in twelfth grade, they yearn to understand the deeper significance of the two tales.

The students begin to appreciate how both of these fairy tales describe long-protected, childlike aspects of the Russian folk soul. As we have seen in "The Firebird," Ivan is the child who simply cannot keep his hands off others' belongings, and whose remorse doesn't prevent him from repeating this transgression at the very next opportunity. He would never have deserved the good fortune that the wolf orchestrates for him had Ivan not experienced the "sleep of death." Somehow, that spiritual suffering ennobles Ivan enough to be worthy of his ultimate reward. Yet he would have "slept forever" had it not been for the wolf, a phrase that leads students to the conclusion that the wolf must signify some awakening quality in the human being. One senior ventured that the wolf's role might represent the same intellectual development all people undergo when they grow from dreamy children into more conscious young adults.

Vasilisa's childlike quality is accentuated by her doll and by the small, pure-hearted kindnesses she shows Baba Yaga's dog, cat, birch tree and gate, all of whom are instrumental in Vasilisa's escape. Yet for Waldorf seniors who grew up on fairy tales, the most distinctive feature of "Vasilisa" is the remarkable ending. Nearly every other fairy tale ends with the wedding of the prince and princess, the union of male and female principles. However, no prince appears to unite with Vasilisa; instead, she lives out her days with her father! What better picture exists of the Russian soul wishing to remain, spiritually speaking, in a virginal state, shielded from those forces that have plunged humanity into the rational and materialistic mindset so characteristic of the West in the past six hundred years.

Seniors are also intrigued by the striking images connected to death and rebirth in the two stories. In "Vasilisa," the skull is both a destroyer (its searing light reduces the sisters and stepmother to ashes) and renewer; from the buried skull, a beautiful rosebush sprouts. Students recognize that the wolf serves the same dual function in "The Firebird." First he is the instrument of death when he devours Ivan's horse; later he restores Ivan to life. Both skull and clever wolf seem to bear a close relationship to thinking, the capacity that can either "destroy" the unity of the world through endless analysis and dissection, or restore it to wholeness by "seeing into the life of things."

The other feature of the two tales that seniors often mention is the suffering that threads through the two tales. Of course suffering can be found in all fairy and folk tales, but for Russians it seems to be almost a defining feature of existence. In 1978, Nobel Prize winner and Russian exile Alexander Solzhenitsyn delivered his famous Harvard Address, entitled "A World Split Apart." In his talk, he alludes to this capacity of the Russian soul:

> I could not recommend your society in its present state as an ideal for the transformation of ours. Through intense suffering our country has now achieved a spiritual development of such intensity that the Western system in its present state of spiritual exhaustion does not look attractive.
>
> A fact which cannot be disputed is the weakening of human beings in the West while in the East they are becoming firmer and stronger. We have been through a spiritual training far in advance of Western experience. Life's complexity and mortal weight have produced stronger, deeper and more interesting characters than those produced by standardized Western well-being.[167]

Solzhenitsyn could speak with some authority on the subject, having suffered through a dozen years in the Soviet gulag system of forced labor camps and internal exile before his banishment to the West. However, for young people raised in a culture that values comfort and convenience over adversity and exertion,

Solzhenitsyn's critique of Western values often comes as a shock. Some seniors mistakenly believe that Solzhenitsyn is attacking the very foundations of democracy. Others argue that his assessment extends to only those excesses of a free society: a ravenous media, rampant consumerism, and a godless humanism.

> If humanism were right in declaring that man is born to be happy, he would not be born to die. Since his body is doomed to die, his task on earth evidently must be of a more spiritual nature. It cannot be unrestrained enjoyment of everyday life. It cannot be the search for the best ways to obtain material goods and then cheerfully get the most out of them. It has to be the fulfillment of a permanent, earnest duty so that one's life journey may become an experience of moral growth, so that one may leave life a better human being than one started it.[168]

Solzhenitsyn's speech slices right to the heart of many twelfth graders' questions about their own futures. Should they head to college or conservatory or culinary institute right after high school, get on the fast track to a high-paying job and the fulfillment of the American Dream? Should they travel, work on a farm, find some organization that allows them to serve others while they sort out their life's purpose?

If the literature young people read can provide guidance in such matters, then the Russian authors of the nineteenth and twentieth centuries offer a unique counterpoint to the American writers of the same eras. One significant contrast immediately jumps out at twelfth graders: Whereas the American authors write in virtually every genre—essays, journals, letters, poetry, short and long fiction—the Russians rely almost exclusively on poetry and fiction. Why? Because censorship in Tsarist, and then Soviet, Russia was so absolute, so intolerant of voices critical of the regime, that Russian authors had to couch their views in poetic and fictional forms. As the Russian comic Yacob Smirnoff has quipped, only half jokingly, "In our country poetry is really important. They kill people for it here!"

Solzhenitsyn's characterization of his people's spiritual strength, tempered in the crucible of suffering, underscores this key distinction between American and Russian writers. America's authors may have suffered personal losses and private torments, but they could celebrate the boundless possibilities of selfhood largely without fear of imprisonment. However, the incarceration or exile of writers from Pushkin to Irina Ratushinskaya has imbued their work with an intensity that burns brighter than that of their American counterparts. Emerson can observe with a certain illuminating detachment that "the invariable mark of wisdom is to see the miraculous in the common." Yet when Irina Ratushinskaya scratches out verses on bars of soap in a Soviet prison on the same subject, the words are electrifying:

> And I'll be asked: what helped us to live
> When there was neither letters nor any news—only walls
> And the cold of the cell, and the blather of official lies,
> And the sickening promises made in exchange for betrayal.
> And I will tell of the first beauty I saw in captivity.
> A frost-covered window!
> No spy holes, nor walls,
> Nor cell bars, nor the long-endured pain—
> Only a blue radiance on a tiny pane of glass...
> Such a gift can only be received once,
> And perhaps it is only needed once.[169]

Thoreau can spend a night in the local Concord jail and crow about how unfettered he feels, while Dostoevsky is arrested for his involvement in an underground press, endures solitary confinement for eight months, is condemned to death and then roused from his cot in the predawn of a biting cold December day. With the sun rising red on the snow, he joins other prisoners in a cart that rattles a few miles to a familiar square. He is given a white linen shirt with long sleeves, lined up before a firing squad and shivers while he waits to die—for ten, twenty, forty minutes—before a last-minute reprieve comes. While he spends the next four years in a Siberian prison, with bare planks for a bed and cockroaches in the soup, he experiences what he calls "the joy of resurrection, something like a song," an untapped reservoir of spiritual energy.

Given such travails, it is not so surprising that Russian literature possesses an unsurpassed intensity. Of all the short works twelfth graders read in this course—Pushkin's "The Bronze Horseman," Gogol's "The Overcoat," the "Grand Inquisitor" scene from Dostoevksy's *The Brothers Karamazov*, Soloviev's *Anti-Christ*—none addresses this idea of the transformative power of suffering as illuminatingly as Leo Tolstoy's "The Death of Ivan Ilych."

Tolstoy opens with Ivan Ilych's funeral, then flashes back to the events of his life that led to his death at age forty-five. "Ivan Ilych's life had been most simple and most ordinary and therefore most terrible."[170] First by birth and then by choice, he follows the conventional formula to success in his career, if not entirely in his personal life.

> Even when he was at the School of Law, he was just what he remained for the rest of his life: a capable, cheerful, good-natured, and sociable man, though strict in the fulfillment of what he considered to be his duty: and he considered his duty to be what was so considered by those in authority.[171]

Ivan Ilych reaches all the accepted milestones of one's life with an eye towards correctness. He wears clothing from the most fashionable tailor, marries a woman of good breeding, becomes a respected magistrate who operates with a "dignified aloofness," and becomes a father. Only when his wife begins making demands on his time does he notice a certain unpleasantness creep into his days. "As his wife grew more irritable and exacting, Ivan Ilych transferred the center of gravity of his life more and more to his work."[172] By retreating increasingly into his official duties, he manages to largely ignore the "ocean of veiled hostility" spreading between him and his wife. Outwardly at least, they maintain the charade of a happy and fulfilling relationship.

Passed over for a promotion, Ivan Ilych resolves to secure a better-paying position, which he does with relative ease. The family moves into a more spacious and elegant house in a more prestigious neighborhood; they entertain dinner guests, exchange chitchat, and, on the whole, "his life ran its course as he believed it should do: easily, pleasantly, and decorously."[173]

However, Ivan Ilych's sham of a life slowly unravels as his health deserts him. A seemingly minor fall from a ladder leads to chronic pain in his side. He visits doctors, takes mountains of medications, lies awake at night trying to wish the gnawing pain away. Gradually he begins to confront the terrifying prospect of his own mortality.

> When I am not, what will there be? There will be nothing. Then where shall I be when I am no more? Can this be dying? No, I don't want to! ...It is impossible that all men have been doomed to suffer this awful horror.[174]

Yet suffer he does, partly from the incessant pain, but as much from the "deception, the lie, that he was not dying but was simply ill, and that he only need keep quiet and undergo a treatment and then something very good would result."[175] Only the presence of an unassuming peasant named Gerasim, who exudes health and vitality, gives Ivan Ilych any comfort. He feels immeasurably soothed when Gerasim props Ivan's legs up on the peasant's shoulders. Otherwise, Ivan Ilych wallows in self-pity, despair and bitterness.

Towards the end of his suffering, Ivan Ilych finally begins the critically important task of self-reflection. He asks of God the reason for all this torment, then grows quiet to hear an answer.

> It was as though he were listening not to an audible voice but to the voice of his soul, to the current of thoughts arising within him. "What is it you want?" was the first clear conception capable of expression in words that he heard.
> "What do I want? To live and not to suffer," he answered.
> "To live? How?" asked his inner voice.
> "Why, to live as I used to—well and pleasantly."
> "As you lived before, well and pleasantly?" the voice repeated.[176]

In this manner of inward listening, Ivan Ilych begins to examine the trajectory of his past life; for the first time, he sees the triviality, the falsehood and worthlessness of all that he had previously prized. Soon after this realization, Ivan Ilych enters a final stage of suffering; he struggles to escape from a suffocating black sack,

> into which he was being thrust by an invisible, resistless force. He struggled as a man condemned to death struggles in the hands of the executioner, knowing that he cannot save himself. And every moment he felt that despite all his efforts he was drawing nearer and nearer to what terrified him.[177]

During the last three days of his life, Ivan Ilych screams in nonstop pain; one could hear it through two closed doors. Yet inside himself, a strange calm descends as he finally falls through the bottom of the sack and finds, not death, but light. This discovery occurs at the same moment his tearful son takes Ivan's hand and kisses it.

> He opened his eyes, looked at his son, and felt
> sorry for him. ...He was sorry for them, he must
> act so as not to hurt them: release them and free
> himself from these sufferings. "How good and how
> simple!" he thought. "And the pain?" he asked
> himself. "What has become of it?"...
> "Yes, here it is. Well, what of it? Let the pain be."
> "And death...where is it?"
> He sought his former accustomed fear of death
> and did not find it. "Where is death? What death?"
> There was no fear because there was no death.[178]

Ivan Ilych's final insight reaffirms a truth that seniors have encountered repeatedly, both in the circumstances of their own lives and in the literature they have read. Young people learn all too soon that they cannot escape some measure of suffering. It is the crucible that life provides for self-transformation. It is also the experience that, if they are able to reach beyond their own personal pain, can unite them with every other human being, can endow them with the gift of compassion. That act of transformation is why Dostoevsky, who suffered through years in a hellish Siberian prison camp and his own lifelong epileptic seizures, could say in his famous Pushkin Address, "To become a true Russian ...means only to become the brother of all men."[179]

A Final Lesson: The Power of Transformation

Last spring a class of twelfth graders culminated their high school careers by undertaking a dramatic production of *Metamorphoses*, writer/director Mary Zimmerman's adaptation of Ovid's classical myths. At first a number of seniors resisted the idea of staging a play that seemed so far removed from modern life. However, once they really read the script, they agreed that each of the tales Zimmerman chose to dramatize resonated with particularly contemporary relevance. The story of Midas, for example, whose own daughter is turned into a golden statue because of his greed, casts new light on the recent spate of incidents involving corporate and governmental greed. The scene with Phaeton, son of Apollo, who crashes his father's sun-bearing chariot while trying to ride across the sky, becomes a psychotherapy session exploring modern-day issues regarding teenagers' need for independence.

Other segments of the play are less contemporary than they are timeless. Orpheus travels to the Underworld to find his beloved Eurydice, only to lose her forever because he cannot refrain from looking back at her as they cross the threshold between the dead and the living. This story is layered with young people's all-too-familiar, often overpowering impulses of desire, impatience and inconsolability. Yet another tale portrays the absurd tactics some individuals employ to attract a mate. Vertumnus, the Roman god of the seasons, dons one ridiculous and ineffectual disguise after another to impress the object of his affections—the lovely wood nymph Pomona. Only after she chides him into foregoing his masquerade and appearing as his true self does he win her heart—yet another transparent allegory that is not lost on young people.

What unifies all these stories is the element of transformation that lies at the center of each one. Two lovers, separated by death, find new life when they turn into seabirds. Another character, tormented by Hunger for his insolence to the gods, becomes his own last supper. In each scene during the entire production, the young actors playing these roles faced the test of utterly transforming themselves, not only into mythological characters, but from mothers into little girls, from gods into paupers, from human beings into water, trees, solid gold.

The extremity of some of the metamorphoses only seemed to augment the truth that kept breaking through during rehearsals. Whether these students believed in divine aid or not, they experienced in the stories the power of transformation that is both the great prize and the great price of being human. As one of the seniors remarked, the good news is that life continually offers us opportunities to grow. The bad news is that we don't often trust, or even recognize, these moments.

Young people can experience life-threatening, psychic and emotional anguish when they get "stuck," when they believe that the despair they are feeling is never going to go away, that things will never change. In the play, poor, young Myrrha faces a lifetime of unbearable, searing guilt for tricking her father into sleeping with her. After imploring the gods to "change me; make me something else; transform me entirely; let me step out of my own heart,"[180] she wades into a stream and melts away. This is one form of metamorphosis—the life-negating escape that looks at times like an appealing alternative to perpetual pain. Yet the play ends with another transformation of the most life-affirming kind.

Baucis and Philemon have lived as husband and wife into their old age. They are visited by two gods dressed as beggars, who have descended to earth to look for truly kindhearted people. After the gods have had numerous doors shut in their faces, Baucis and Philemon offer to share with their guests their meager fare. For their generosity, the couple is given a single wish. The couple decides that rather than riches or eternal youth, they simply wish to die at the same time. "I'd hate to see my wife's grave," says Philemon, "or have her weep at mine."[181]

The gods grant their wish. Baucis and Philemon grow into even older age together; then one day they discover that they are sprouting leaves, that their limbs are beginning to twist into intertwining branches. They just have time to say farewell to one another as the bark covers their mouths. In Zimmerman's play, the narrators ringing the actors explain that, at night, you can still hear

> stirring in the intermingled branches of the trees above, the ardent prayer of Baucis and Philemon.
> They whisper: 'Let me die the moment my love dies.'
> They whisper, 'Let me not outlive my capacity to love.'
> They whisper, 'Let me die still loving, and so, never die.'[182]

This is the final lesson these young people can learn from Ovid's tales; indeed, from all of the stories that portray the human condition. Like Anne Frank, Odysseus, Gilgamesh, Parzival, Prospero, the Ancient Mariner, Ivan Ilych and countless others, adolescents can see that love remains the most transformative force in life. Even Midas, the embodiment of people's basest, most materialistic impulses, comes to this truth in the very last scene of *Metamorphoses*. To free his daughter of the golden imprisonment he had brought down on them both, he has walked to the ends of the earth to find a pool that reflects the light of the stars. There he stoops, in exhaustion and humility, to wash his hands. In that moment, like a miracle, his daughter is restored. So in reading the stories of humanity that are like earthly pools reflecting heavenly light, young people, too, are restored, ever and again.

Endnotes
1. William Gibson, *The Miracle Worker* (New York: Pocket Books, 1988), pp. 101–102.
2. Neil Postman, *Amusing Ourselves to Death* (New York: Penguin Books, 1986), p. vii.
3. David Elkind, "The Reality of Virtual Stress," *CIO Magazine* (Fall 2003), http://www.cio.com/archive/092203/elind.html?printversion=yes>.
4. Christopher Clouder and David Mitchell, *Rudolf Steiner's Observations on Adolescence* (Fair Oaks, CA: AWSNA Publications, 2001), p. 129.
5. Hermann Baravalle, *Waldorf Education in America* (Spring Valley: Parker Courtney Press, 1998), p. 34.
6. Sophocles, *The Oedipus Plays of Sophocles*, tr. Paul Roche (Meridian: New York, 1996), pp. 59–60.
7. Ibid., p. 82.
8. Lorraine Hansberry, *A Raisin in the Sun* (New York: Random House, 1987), p. 51.
9. Ralph Waldo Emerson, *Selections from Ralph Waldo Emerson*, ed. Stephen Whicher (New York: Houghton Mifflin, 1960), p. 36.
10. Op. cit., Clouder and Mitchell, p. 105.
11. Op. cit., Sophocles, pp. 72–74.
12. George Bush, in a speech given on April 3, 2004, www.innocentenglish.com/funnybloopers mistakes-quotes/funniest-bushisms.html.
13. Ibid., August 5, 2004.
14. Rudolf Steiner, *A Modern Art of Education* (Great Barrington: Anthroposophic Press, 1961), p. 175.
15. Herman Melville, *Moby Dick* (Berkeley and Los Angeles: Arion Press, 1979), p. 3.
16. Ibid.
17. Ibid., p. 186.
18. Ibid., p. 432.
19. Ibid., p. 434.
20. Ibid., p. 329.
21. Rudolf Steiner, *The Work of the Angels in Man's Astral Body* (London: The Anthroposophical Publishing Company, 1960), p. 4.
22. Forrest Carter, *The Education of Little Tree* (Albuquerque: University of New Mexico Press, 1986), p. 57.

23. Ibid., p. 29.
24. Dave Randall, "The Tall Tale of Little Tree and the Cherokee Who Was Really a Klansman," *The Independent* (September 1, 2002), news.independent.co.uk/media/article175400.ece.
25. Anne Frank, *The Diary of Anne Frank* (New York: Bantam, 1993), p. 208.
26. Ibid., p. 137.
27. Ibid., p. 256.
28. Ibid., p. 222.
29. Homer, *The Odyssey*, tr. Fitzgerald (New York: Doubleday and Co., 1963), p. 160.
30. Ibid., p. 236.
31. Thomas Arp, *Perrine's Sound and Sense* (New York: Harcourt Brace,1997), p. 15.
32. Ibid., p. 170.
33. Wendell Berry, "The Wild Geese," *Collected Poems* (New York: North Point Press, 1985), pp. 155–156.
34. Shadrach Woods, "The Boy and the Dove," *The Burning Bush*, Green Meadow Waldorf School Literary Magazine (Spring Valley: Mercury Press, 1987), p. 7.
35. Eric Shurtleff, "My Secret Place," student assignment, 1992.
36. Frances Pharr, "The Hatching," *The Burning Bush*, Green Meadow Waldorf School Literary Magazine (Spring Valley: Mercury Press, 1996), p. 33.
37. Laura Fisher, "The Plum," *The Burning Bush*, Green Meadow Waldorf School Literary Magazine (Spring Valley: Mercury Press, 1985), p. 13.
38. Linda Sussman, *The Speech of the Grail* (Hudson, NY: Lindisfarne, 2000), p. 117.
39. *Gilgamesh,* tr. Herbert Mason (New York: New American Library, 1972), p. 20.
40. Ibid., p. 16.
41. Ibid., p. 17.
42. Ibid., p. 18.
43. Ibid., p. 24.
44. Ibid., p. 30.
45. Ibid., p. 59.
46. Ibid., p. 60.
47. Ibid., p. 53.

48. Ibid., p. 66.
49. Ibid., p. 74.
50. Ibid., p. 84.
51. Ibid., p. 92.
52. Ibid., p. 82.
53. Ibid., p. 84.
54. Ibid., p. 49.
55. Ibid., p. 80.
56. Dante Alighieri, *The Divine Comedy: Volume 1: Inferno*, tr. Mark Musa (New York: Penguin, 2002), ll. 1–3, Canto I, p. 67.
57. Ibid., ll. 35–36, Canto III, p. 90.
58. Ibid., l. 114, Canto VII, p. 133.
59. Ibid., ll. 16–18, Canto VI, p. 122.
60. Ibid, l. 115, Canto XII, p. 177.
61. Ibid., l. 103, Canto XII, p. 179.
62. Ibid., ll. 12–15, Canto XXXIV, pp. 379–380.
63. Op. cit., Arp, p. 91.
64. Wolfram Von Eschenbach, *Parzival*, tr. Helen Mustard and Charles Passage (London, England: Penguin, 1980), p. 78.
65. Ibid., p. 94.
66. Ibid., p. 129.
67. Ibid., p. 138.
68. Ibid., pp. 169–170.
69. Ibid., p. 134.
70. Ibid., p. 178.
71. Ibid., p. 177.
72. Albert Huffstickler, "The Edge of Doubt," *The Certitude of Laundromats* (Austin, TX: Jamming Staplers Press, 1995).
73. Op. cit., Von Eschenbach, p. 361.
74. Ibid., p. 390.
75. Ibid., p. 415.
76. William Shakespeare, *Hamlet* (New York: Washington Square Press,1994), I ii 144, p. 29.
77. Ibid., I v 34–35, pp. 57–58.
78. Ibid., II ii 566–587, p. 117.
79. Ibid., II ii 606–608, p. 119.
80. Ibid., III iv 226, p. 183.
81. Ibid., II ii 613, p. 119.
82. Ibid., V ii 520–530, p. 273.

83. Ibid., II ii 388–389, p. 107.
84. Ibid., V ii 218–221, pp. 271–272.
85. Ibid., V i 84–204, p. 251.
86. Ibid., II ii 323, p. 103.
87. Ibid., III i 138, p. 131.
88. Ibid., I ii 139–140, p. 29.
89. William Shakespeare, *The Tempest* (New York: Washington Square Press, 1994), I ii 417–418, p. 37.
90. Ibid., I ii 552, p. 47.
91. Ibid., I ii 542–555, p. 45.
92. Op. cit., Shakespeare, *Hamlet*, III iv, l. 99–102, p. 117.
93. Op. cit., Shakespeare, *The Tempest*, III iii 70–101, pp. 113–115.
94. Ibid., V i 17–24, pp. 145–147.
95. Ibid., 27–40, p. 147.
96. Ibid., 330–331, p. 165.
97. Ibid., 351–352, p. 167.
98. Ibid., 24–26, p.147.
99. Ibid., 50–55, pp. 147–149.
100. Ibid., 59–66, p. 150.
101. Ibid., Epilogue 1–18, pp. 169–171.
102. Ibid., V i 253–254, p. 161.
103. Rudolf Steiner, "Youth's Search in Nature" (Spring Valley, NY: Mercury Press, 1984).
104. William Wordsworth, "The World Is Too Much with Us," *The Norton Anthology of Poetry*, eds. Margaret Ferguson, Mary Jo Salter and Jon Stallworthy (New York: W.W. Norton, 1997), p. 424.
105. Harold Bloom and Lionel Trilling, *Romantic Poetry and Prose* (New York: Oxford University Press, 1973), p. 595.
106. Ibid., p. 596.
107. Ibid.
108. Ibid.
109. Ibid., p. 597.
110. Ibid., p. 149.
111. Ibid., p. 147.
112. Ibid.
113. Ibid., p. 257.
114. Ibid., p. 240.
115. Ibid., p. 242.
116. Ibid., p. 245.

117. Ibid.
118. Ibid., p. 246.
119. *The British Critic*, February 1819.
120. Sydney Smith, *The Edinburgh Review*, January 1820.
121. Op. cit., Emerson, p. 54.
122. Ibid., p. 68.
123. Ibid., p. 79.
124. Ibid., p. 149.
125. Ibid., pp. 149, 159.
126. Ibid., p. 158.
127. Ibid., p. 147.
128. Walt Whitman, *Leaves of Grass* (New York: Bantam, 1983), p. 23.
129. Henry David Thoreau, *Walden and Civil Disobedience* (New York: Penguin, 1983), p. 219.
130. Ibid., p. 65.
131. Ibid., pp. 222, 229, 234.
132. Ibid., pp. 8, 14.
133. Ibid., p. 53.
134. Ibid., p. 218.
135. Ibid., p. 150.
136. Ibid., p. 148.
137. Ibid., p. 150.
138. Jonathan Edwards, "Sinners in the Hands of an Angry God" (P&R Publishing, 1992).
139. Nathaniel Hawthorne, *Hawthorne's Short Stories* (New York: Vintage, 1946), p. 177.
140. Ibid., p. 178.
141. Op cit., Whitman, p. 22.
142. Ibid., p. 47.
143. Ibid., p. 37.
144. Ibid., p. 66.
145. Ibid., p. 42.
146. Ibid., p. 70.
147. Ibid., p. 68.
148. Thomas Wentworth Higginson, "Emily Dickinson's Letters," *The Atlantic Monthly* (Volume 68, Issue 408, October 1891), p. 447.
149. Emily Dickinson, *The Laurel Poetry Series*, ed. John Malcolm Brinnin (New York: Dell Publishing Co., 1960), p. 55.
150. Ibid., p. 40.

151. Op. cit., Higginson, p. 453.
152. Ibid., p. 50.
153. Op. cit., Shakespeare, *Hamlet*, p. 99.
154. Op. cit., Bloom and Trilling, p. 27.
155. Op. cit., Hawthorne, p. 167.
156. Johann Wolfgang von Goethe, *Goethe's Faust*, tr. Walter Kaufman (New York: Anchor Books, 1961), pp. 247–249.
157. Ibid., p. 181.
158. Ibid., p. 187.
159. Ibid., p. 145.
160. *The Holy Bible, King James Version, 1611 Edition* (Peabody, MA: Hendrickson Publishing, 2003) Matthew 22:21.
161. Op. cit., Shakespeare, *Hamlet,* II ii 318–332, pp. 101–103.
162. Op. cit., Dickinson, p. 94.
163. Op. cit., Goethe, p. 403.
164. Ron Rosenbaum, "Staring into the Heart of the Heart of Darkness," (*New York Times Magazine*, June 4, 1995), p. 39.
165. Op. cit., Goethe, p. 87.
166. Marianna Mayer, *Baba Yaga and Vasilisa the Brave* (New York: HarperCollins, 1994).
167. Alexander Solzhenitsyn, "A World Split Apart," Harvard Address, 1978, www.columbia.edu/cu/augustine/arch/solzhenitsyn/harvard1978.htm.
168. Ibid.
169. Irina Ratushinskaya, *No, I'm Not Afraid* (Chester Springs, PA: Dufour Editions 1992).
170. Leo Tolstoy, *The Death of Ivan Ilych* (New York: Bantam Classics, 1981), p. 104.
171. Ibid., p. 105.
172. Ibid., p. 110.
173. Ibid., p. 117.
174. Ibid., p. 130.
175. Ibid., p. 137.
176. Ibid., p. 147.
177. Ibid., p. 154.
178. Ibid., p. 155.
179. Fyodor Dostoevsky, "Pushkin Address," *The Portable Nineteenth Century Russian Reader*, ed. George Gibian (New York: Penguin Books, 1993), p. 434.

180. Mary Zimmerman, *Metamorphoses: A Play* (Evanston, IL: Northwestern University Press, 2002), p. 60.
181. Ibid., p. 82.
182. Ibid., p. 14.

BIBLIOGRAPHY

Alighieri, Dante. *The Divine Comedy, Volume 1: Inferno*, tr. Mark Musa, New York: Penguin, 2002.

Anonymous. *The British Critic*, London, February 1819.

Baravalle, Hermann. *Waldorf Education in America*, Spring Valley: Parker Courtney Press, 1998.

Barfield, Owen. *Saving the Appearances,* Hanover, NH: University Press of New England,1988.

Berry, Wendell. "The Wild Geese," *The Selected Poems of Wendell Berry*, Washington, DC: Counterpoint Press, 1998.

Blake, William. "London," *The Oxford Anthology of English Literature, Volume IV: Romantic Poetry and Prose*, Oxford: Oxford University Press, 1973.

Brooks, Gwendolyn. "We Real Cool," *Sound and Sense: An Introduction to Poetry*, eds. Laurence Perrine and Thomas Arp, New York: Harcourt, 1991.

Burleson, Patricia. "The History and Artistry of Haiku," *Japan Digest*, October 1998.

Carter, Forrest. *The Education of Little Tree*, Albuquerque: University of New Mexico Press, 1986.

Coleridge, Samuel Taylor. "The Rime of the Ancient Mariner," "Kubla Khan," *The Oxford Anthology of English Literature, Volume IV: Romantic Poetry and Prose*, Oxford: Oxford University Press, 1973.

Dickinson, Emily. *The Complete Poems of Emily Dickinson*, Boston: Back Bay Books, 1976.

Edwards, Jonathan. "Sinners in the Hands of an Angry God," P&R Publishing, 1992.

Elkind, David. "The Reality of Virtual Stress," *CIO Magazine*, Fall 2003.

Emerson, Ralph Waldo. *Selections from Ralph Waldo Emerson*, ed. Stephen Whicher, New York: Houghton Mifflin, 1960.

Fisher, Laura. "The Plum," *The Burning Bush*, Green Meadow Waldorf School Literary Magazine, Spring Valley, NY: Mercury Press, 1985.

Frank, Anne. *The Diary of Anne Frank*, New York: Bantam, 1993.

Frost, Robert. "Fire and Ice," *Sound and Sense: An Introduction to Poetry*, eds. Laurence Perrine and Thomas Arp, New York: Harcourt, 1991.

Frye, Northrop. *The Great Code*, Orlando, FL: Harcourt, 1983.

Gibson, William. *The Miracle Worker*, New York: Pocket Books, 1988.

Gilgamesh, tr. Herbert Mason, New York: New American Library, 1972.

Goethe, Wolfgang. *Faust*, tr. Walter Kaufman, New York: Anchor Books, 1961.

Hansberry, Lorraine. *A Raisin in the Sun,* New York: Random House, 1987.

Hawthorne, Nathaniel. *Short Stories*, New York: Vintage, 1946

Holy Bible, King James Version, 1611 Edition, The. Peabody, MA: Hendrickson Publishing, 2003.

Homer. *The Odyssey*, tr. Fitzgerald, New York: Doubleday and Co., 1963.

Huffstickler, Albert. "The Edge of Doubt" *The Certitude of Laundromats*. Austin, TX: Jamming Staplers Press, 1995.

Kubler-Ross, Elisabeth. *On Death and Dying*, New York: Macmillan Publishing Company, 1969.

Mayer, Marianna. *Baba Yaga and Vasilisa the Brave,* New York: HarperCollins, 1994.

Melville, Herman. *Moby Dick,* Berkeley and Los Angeles: Arion Press, 1979.

Mitchell, David and Christopher Clouder. *Rudolf Steiner's Observations on Adolescence,* Fair Oaks, CA: AWSNA Publications, 2001.

Pharr, Frances. "The Hatching," *The Burning Bush*, Green Meadow Waldorf School Literary Magazine, Spring Valley, NY: Mercury Press, 1996.

Postman Neil. *Amusing Ourselves to Death,* New York: Penguin Books, 1986.

Ratushinskaya, Irina. *No, I'm Not Afraid*, Chester Springs, PA: Dufour Editions, 1992.

Rosenbaum, Ron. "Staring into the Heart of the Heart of Darkness," *New York Times Magazine*, June 4, 1995.

Shakespeare, William. *A Midsummer Night's Dream,* New York: Washington Square Press, 1992.

_____. *Hamlet,* New York: Washington Square Press, 1994.

_____. *The Tempest,* New York: Washington Square Press, 2004.

Smith, Sydney. *The Edinburgh Review,* 1818.

Solzhenitsyn, Alexander. "A World Split Apart," Harvard Address, 1978.

Sophocles. *The Oedipus Plays of Sophocles,* tr. Paul Roche, New York: Meridian, 1996.

Spirin, Gennady. *The Tale of the Firebird,* New York: Philomel, 2002.

Steiner, Rudolf. *A Modern Art of Education,* Great Barrington, MA: Anthroposophic Press, 1961.

_____. *The Spiritual Ground of Education*, Great Barrington, MA: Anthroposophic Press, 1991.

_____. *The Work of the Angels in Man's Astral Body*, London: The Anthroposophical Publishing Company, 1960.

_____. "Youth's Search in Nature," Spring Valley, NY: Mercury Press, 1984.

Sussman, Linda. *The Speech of the Grail,* Hudson, NY: Lindisfarne, 2000.

Thoreau, Henry David. *Walden and Civil Disobedience*, New York: Penguin, 1983.

Tolstoy, Leo. *The Death of Ivan Ilych,* New York: Bantam Classics, 1981.

Von Eschenbach, Wolfram. *Parzival,* tr. Helen Mustard and Charles Passage, London: Penguin, 1980.

Walsh, David, Douglas A. Gentile, Erin Walsh and Nat Bennett. "MediaWise® Video Game Report Card," National Institute on Media and the Family, November 28, 2006.

Whitman, Walt. *Leaves of Grass,* New York: Bantam, 1983.

Williams, William Carlos. "The Red Wheelbarrow," *Sound and Sense: An Introduction to Poetry*, eds. Laurence Perrine and Thomas Arp, New York: Harcourt, 1991.

Woods, Shadrach. "The Boy and the Dove," *The Burning Bush*, Green Meadow Waldorf School Literary Magazine, Spring Valley, NY: Mercury Press, 1986.

Wordsworth, William. "Ode: Intimations of Immortality," "The World Is Too Much with Us,""Preface to Lyrical Ballads," "Tintern Abbey," *The Oxford Anthology of English Literature, Volume IV: Romantic Poetry and Prose*, Oxford: Oxford University Press, 1973.

Zimmerman, Mary. *Metamorphoses: A Play*, Evanston, IL: Northwestern University Press, 2002.

Dedication

This book is dedicated to my parents—Sol Sloan, who lived a life worthy of a master storyteller; Polly Sloan, still in love with the power of words, especially rhyme; my brothers Gary, Steve, and Bennett, whose interweaving stories have been so much of mine; my wife Christine, my muse and "a-muse" ; and our children, Joshua, Benjamin, Caitlin, and Zachary, the happiest, ever-after ending we could imagine.

www.ingramcontent.com/pod-product-compliance
Lightning Source LLC
Chambersburg PA
CBHW031259110426
42743CB00041B/741